TRANSPORTATION INFRASTRUCTURE - ROADS, HIGHWAYS, BRIDGES, AIRPORTS AND MASS TRANSIT SERIES

SURFACE TRANSPORTATION: INFRASTRUCTURE, ENVIRONMENTAL ISSUES AND SAFETY

TRANSPORTATION INFRASTRUCTURE - ROADS, HIGHWAYS, BRIDGES, AIRPORTS AND MASS TRANSIT SERIES

America's Bridges???
Evan N. Kantwell (Editor)
2009. ISBN: 978-1-60456-097-8

Strengthening Historic Covered Bridges to Carry Modern Traffic
Martin B. Reece
2009. ISBN: 978-1-60692-581-2

Surface Transportation: Infrastructure, Environmental Issues and Safety
Keith A. Libermann (Editor)
2009. ISBN: 978-1-60692-357-3

TRANSPORTATION INFRASTRUCTURE - ROADS, HIGHWAYS, BRIDGES, AIRPORTS AND MASS TRANSIT SERIES

SURFACE TRANSPORTATION: INFRASTRUCTURE, ENVIRONMENTAL ISSUES AND SAFETY

KEITH A. LIBERMANN
EDITOR

Nova Science Publishers, Inc.
New York

For permission to use material from this book please contact us:
Telephone 631-231-7269; Fax 631-231-8175
Web Site: http://www.novapublishers.com

Additional color graphics may be available in the e-book version of this book.

LIBRARY OF CONGRESS CATALOGING-IN-PUBLICATION DATA

Surface transportation : infrastructure, environmental issues, and safety / editor, Keith A. Libermann.
p. cm.
Includes bibliographical references and index.
ISBN: 978-1-60692-357-3 (hardcover : alk. paper)
1. Roads--Finance--Government Policy--United States. 2. Transportation, Automotive--Government Policy--United States. 3. Federal aid to transportation--United States. 4. Transportation, Automotive--Environmental aspects--United States. 5. Traffic safety--United States. I. Libermann, Keith A. II. United States. Government Accountability Office. III. United States. Congressional Budget Office.
HE336.E3S965 2009
388.10973--dc22

2009028865

Published by Nova Science Publishers, Inc. ✝ New York

CONTENTS

PREFACE

This book provides an overview of the federal role in surface transportation and the goals and structures of federal programs. Since federal financing for the interstate system was established in 1956, the federal role in surface transportation has expanded to include broader goals, more programs, and a variety of program structures. The nation has reached a critical juncture with its current surface transportation policies and programs. Demand has outpaced the capacity of the system, resulting in increased congestion. In addition, without significant changes in funding levels or planned spending, the Highway Trust Fund - the major source of federal highway and transit funding - is projected to incur significant deficits in the years ahead. Exacerbating concerns about the solvency of the Highway Trust Fund is the federal government's bleak fiscal condition and outlook. As a result, other federal revenue sources may not be available to help solve the nation's current transportation challenges. Given the scope of needed transformation, it may be necessary to shift policies and programs incrementally or on a pilot basis to gain practical lessons for a coherent, sustainable, and effective national program and financing structure to best serve the nation for the 21st century.

Chapter 1 - Surface transportation programs need to be reexamined in the context of the nation's current unsustainable fiscal path. Surface transportation programs are particularly ready for review as the Highway Trust Fund faces a fiscal imbalance at a time when both congestion and travel demand are growing. As you requested, this report (1) provides an overview of the federal role in surface transportation and the goals and structures of federal programs, (2) summarizes GAO's conclusions about the structure and performance of these programs, and (3) provides principles to assess options for focusing future surface transportation programs. GAO's study is based on prior GAO reports, stakeholder reports and interviews, Department of Transportation documents, and the views of transportation experts.

Chapter 2 – This is a testimony of Jayetta Z. Hecker, Director, Physical Infrastructure Issues, before the Committee on Finance, United States Senate.

Chapter 3 – This is a testimony of Robert A. Sunshine, Deputy Director, Public Spending on Surface Transportation Infrastructure, before the Committee on the Budget, United States House of Representative.

In: Surface Transportation
Editor: Keith A. Libermann, PP: 1-79
ISBN: 978-1-60692-357-3

Chapter 1

SURFACE TRANSPORTATION: RESTRUCTURED FEDERAL APPROACH NEEDED FOR MORE FOCUSED, PERFORMANCE-BASED, AND SUSTAINABLE PROGRAMS

Government Accountability Office

WHY GAO DID THIS STUDY

Surface transportation programs need to be reexamined in the context of the nation's current unsustainable fiscal path. Surface transportation programs are particularly ready for review as the Highway Trust Fund faces a fiscal imbalance at a time when both congestion and travel demand are growing. As you requested, this report (1) provides an overview of the federal role in surface transportation and the goals and structures of federal programs, (2) summarizes GAO's conclusions about the structure and performance of these programs, and (3) provides principles to assess options for focusing future surface transportation programs. GAO's study is based on prior GAO reports, stakeholder reports and interviews, Department of Transportation documents, and the views of transportation experts.

What GAO Recommends

Congress should consider reexamining and refocusing surface transportation programs so that they: (1) have goals with direct links to an identified federal interest and role, (2) make grantees more accountable through more performance-based links between funding and program outcomes, (3) use tools and approaches that emphasize the return on the federal investment, and (4) address the current imbalance between federal surface transportation revenues and spending. DOT generally agreed with the information in this report, and provided technical clarifications, which were incorporated as appropriate.

What GAO Found

Since federal financing for the interstate system was established in 1956, the federal role in surface transportation has expanded to include broader goals, more programs, and a variety of program structures. To incorporate additional transportation, environmental and societal goals, federal surface transportation programs have grown in number and complexity. While some of these goals have been incorporated as new grant programs in areas such as transit, highway safety, and motor carrier safety, others have been incorporated as additional procedural requirements for receiving federal aid. Broad program goals, eligibility requirements, and transfer provisions give states and local governments substantial discretion for allocating most highway infrastructure funds. For transit and safety programs, broad basic grant programs are augmented by programs that either require a competitive selection process or use financial incentives to directly target federal funds toward specific goals or safety activities.

Many current programs are not effective at addressing key transportation challenges such as increasing congestion and freight demand. They generally do not meet these challenges because federal goals and roles are unclear, many programs lack links to needs or performance, and the programs often do not employ the best tools and approaches. The goals of current programs are numerous and sometimes conflicting. Furthermore, states' ability to transfer highway infrastructure funds among different programs is so flexible that some program distinctions have little meaning. Moreover, programs often do not employ the best tools and approaches; rigorous economic analysis is not a driving factor in most project selection decisions and tools to make better use of existing infrastructure have not been deployed to their full potential. Modally-stovepiped funding can impede efficient planning and project selection and, according to state officials, congressionally directed spending may limit the states' ability to implement projects and efficiently use transportation funds.

A number of principles can help guide the assessment of options for transforming federal surface transportation programs. These principles include: (1) ensuring goals are well defined and focused on the federal interest, (2) ensuring the federal role in achieving each goal is clearly defined, (3) ensuring accountability for results by entities receiving federal funds, (4) employing the best tools and approaches to emphasize return on targeted federal investment, and (5) ensuring fiscal sustainability. With the sustainability and performance issues of current programs, it is an opportune time for Congress to more clearly define the federal role in transportation and improve progress toward specific, nationally-defined outcomes. Given the scope of needed transformation, it may be necessary to shift policies and programs incrementally or on a pilot basis to gain practical lessons for a coherent, sustainable, and effective national program and financing structure to best serve the nation for the 21st century.

ABBREVIATIONS

AASHTO	American Association of State Highway and Transportation Officials
APTA	American Public Transit Association
CBO	Congressional Budget Office
CDLP	Commercial Driver's License Program
CMAQ	Congestion Mitigation & Air Quality Improvement Program
DOT	Department of Transportation
FHWA	Federal Highway Administration
FMCSA	Federal Motor Carrier Safety Administration
FRA	Federal Railroad Administration
FTA	Federal Transit Administration
GPRA	Government Performance and Results Act
HBRRP	Highway Bridge Replacement and Rehabilitation Program

HSIP	Highway Safety Improvement Program
HTF	Highway Trust Fund
ICC	Interstate Commerce Commission
IM	Interstate Maintenance Program
ISTEA	Intermodal Surface Transportation Efficiency Act
ITS	intelligent transportation systems
Mph	miles per hour
MCSAP	Motor Carrier Safety Assistance Program
MPO	Metropolitan Planning Organizations
NEPA	National Environmental Policy Act of 1969
NHS	National Highway System
NHTSA	National Highway Traffic Safety Administration
RABA	revenue-aligned budget authority
RITA	Research and Innovative Technology Administration
SAFETEA-LU	Safe, Accountable, Flexible, Efficient Transportation Equity Act - A Legacy for Users
STP	Surface Transportation Program
UMTA	Urban Mass Transit Act of 1964

March 6, 2008

The Honorable James Inhofe
Ranking Member
Committee on Environment and Public Works
United States Senate

The Honorable Jim DeMint
United States Senate

Transportation programs, like all areas of federal involvement, need to be viewed in the context of the nation's fiscal position. Long-term fiscal simulations by GAO, the Congressional Budget Office (CBO), and others all show that despite a 3-year decline in the federal government's unified budget deficit, we still face large and growing structural deficits driven by rising health care costs and known demographic trends. As the baby boom generation retires, entitlement programs will grow and require increasing shares of federal spending. Absent significant changes to tax and spending programs and policies, we face a future of unsustainable deficits and debt that threaten to cripple our economy and quality of life.[1] Although the long-term outlook is driven by health care costs, demographics and revenues, other areas of government should also be re-examined. This involves a fundamental reexamination of government programs and commitments by reviewing their results and testing their continued relevance and relative priority for the 21st century. This reexamination offers an opportunity to address emerging needs by eliminating outdated or ineffective programs, more sharply defining the federal role in relation to state and local roles, and modernizing those programs and policies that remain relevant.

The nation's surface transportation programs are particularly ready for reexamination. For example, the Highway Trust Fund (HTF) was created in 1956 to finance the construction of the Interstate Highway System because of the national interest in interstate mobility. That system is now complete. However, the federal highway program's financing and delivery mechanisms have not substantially changed and their continued relevance in the 21st century is unclear. In addition, without significant changes in funding mechanisms or revenue sources, or reductions in planned spending, the HTF is projected to begin incurring significant deficits in the years ahead. As a result, in 2007, we added financing the nation's federal transportation infrastructure to GAO's High Risk List.

Given the need to reexamine all government programs and the importance of a sustainable federal role in the nation's surface transportation system, you asked us to examine the federal approach to surface transportation programs—in particular, those financed by the HTF. This report (1) provides an historical overview of the federal role in surface transportation and the goals and structures of federal surface transportation programs funded by the HTF, (2) summarizes conclusions from our prior work on the structure and performance of these and other federal surface transportation programs, and (3) identifies principles to help assess options for focusing the future federal role and structure of federal surface transportation programs.

To provide an historical overview of the federal role in surface transportation and the goals and structures of federal surface transportation programs funded by the HTF, we drew information from statutes, regulations, budget documents, agency reports, and literature on transportation policy by outside experts. We also interviewed officials in the Office of the Secretary of Transportation and in the relevant Department of Transportation (DOT) modal administrations. To summarize conclusions from our prior work on the structure and performance of federal surface transportation programs, we synthesized relevant GAO reports on specific transportation programs, and reports that looked at broader issues of performance measurement, oversight, grant design, and other related issues. We also reviewed reports and other materials from stakeholder groups and other organizations and sought the views of transportation experts, including those who participated in a forum on transportation challenges convened by the Comptroller General in June 2007. To identify principles to help assess options for focusing the future federal role and the structure of surface transportation programs, we examined principles found in relevant GAO reports on specific transportation programs, and reports that looked at broader issues such as performance measurement, oversight, grant design, and other related issues. We performed our work between April 2007 and February 2008 in accordance with generally accepted government auditing standards. A more extensive discussion of our scope and methodology is in appendix I.

RESULTS IN BRIEF

Since the Federal-Aid Highway Act of 1956 created the modern federal highway program, the federal role in surface transportation has expanded to include broader goals, more programs, and a variety of program structures. Although most surface transportation funds remain dedicated to highway infrastructure, federal surface transportation programs have grown in number and complexity, incorporating additional transportation, environmental, and societal goals. While some of these goals have been incorporated as new grant programs in areas such as transit, highway safety, and motor carrier safety, others have been incorporated as additional procedural requirements for receiving federal aid, such as environmental review and transportation planning requirements. This program expansion has also created a variety of grant structures and federal approaches for establishing priorities and distributing federal funds. Most highway infrastructure funds continue to be distributed to states in accordance with individual grant program formulas and eligibility requirements. However, broad program goals, eligibility requirements, and authority to transfer funds between programs give state and local governments substantial discretion for allocating highway infrastructure funds according to their priorities. Although some transit formula grant programs also give grantees considerable discretion to allocate funds, a portion of transit assistance requires grantees to compete for funding based on specific criteria and goals. Similarly, basic safety formula grant programs are augmented by smaller programs that directly target federal funds to specific goals and actions using financial incentives and penalty provisions. Federal law has also increasingly allocated infrastructure funds through provisions directing spending to specific areas or projects. For example, according to the Transportation Research Board, the most recent surface transportation reauthorization legislation, passed in 2005—the Safe, Accountable, Flexible, Efficient Transportation Equity Act – a Legacy for Users (SAFETEA-LU)—contained over 5,000 dedicated spending provisions. Additionally, state and local government responsibility for oversight has recently increased, as state and local governments have assumed oversight responsibility for the majority of highway infrastructure spending, and federal safety programs have shifted from direct program oversight to a more performance-based approach.

Our summary of our prior conclusions about federal surface transportation programs found that many of these programs are not effective at addressing key transportation challenges such as increasing congestion and growing freight demand because federal goals and roles are unclear, many programs lack links to needs or performance, and the programs in some areas do not employ the best tools and approaches to ensure effective investment decisions. The goals of federal surface transportation programs are numerous and sometimes conflicting, which contributes to a corresponding lack of clarity in the federal role. For example, despite statutes and regulations that call for an intermodal approach that creates connections across modes, there is only one federal program specifically designed for intermodal infrastructure. Most highway funds are distributed through formulas that have only an indirect relationship to needs and no relationship to performance or outcomes. The largest safety and transit grants are also distributed through formulas without regard to performance. However safety grants more likely than highway grants to be focused on goals rather than specific transportation systems, and several highway safety and motor carrier safety grants allocate incentive funds on the basis of performance or states undertaking specific safety-related activities. Since the majority of surface transportation funds are distributed without regard to performance, it is difficult to assess the impact of recent record levels of federal highway expenditures, though congestion has increased in the same period. Mechanisms to link programs to goals also appear insufficient, because particularly in the Federal-Aid Highway Program, federal rules for transferring funds between different highway infrastructure programs are so flexible that the distinctions between individual programs have little meaning. Furthermore, surface transportation programs often do not employ the best tools and approaches to ensure effective investment decisions. Rigorous economic analysis is not a driving factor in most investment decisions by state and local governments—in a survey of state DOTs, 34 cited political support and public opinion as very important factors, whereas 8 said the same of the ratio of benefits to costs. The federal government also does not possess adequate data to assess outcomes or implement performance measures; for example, DOT does not have a central source of data on congestion, even though it has identified congestion as a top priority. While some funds can be transferred between highway and transit programs, modally-stovepiped funding nevertheless impedes efficient planning and project selection. State DOT officials have noted that congressionally directed spending may limit states' ability to implement projects and efficiently use transportation funds. Additionally, tools to make better use of existing infrastructure, such as intelligent transportation systems and congestion pricing, have not been deployed to their full potential. Finally, increases in federal spending for transportation appear to reduce state spending for the same purpose, reducing the return on the federal investment—research estimates that 50 percent of each additional federal grant dollar for the highway program displaces funds that states would otherwise have spent on highways.

Through our prior work on reexamining the base of government, our analysis of existing programs and other prior reports, we identified a number of principles that could help drive reexamination of federal surface transportation programs and an assessment of options for restructuring the federal surface transportation program. These principles include: (1) ensuring goals are well defined and focused on the federal interest, (2) ensuring the federal role in achieving each goal is clearly defined, (3) ensuring accountability for results by entities receiving federal funds, (4) employing the best tools and approaches to emphasize return on targeted federal investment, and (5) ensuring fiscal sustainability. The first step involves identifying issues in which there is a strong federal interest and determining what the federal goals should be related to those issues. Once the federal interest and goals have been identified, the federal role in relation to the states and local governments can be clearly defined. For issues in which there is a strong federal interest, ongoing federal financial support and direct federal involvement could help meet federal goals. But for issues in which there is little or no federal interest, programs and activities may best be devolved to other levels of government. The next step is to ensure accountability for results by incorporating performance objectives, grant incentive or penalty provisions, or more use of competitive selection procedures in awarding grants. Then, in assessing investment decisions, more emphasis could be placed on return on investment and benefit-cost analysis as criteria for comparing alternatives and directing funds. The relationship of investments to national goals also should be considered along with locally-based calculations of benefit and cost. Efficient investment decisions can be facilitated by employing the best tools and approaches, using mechanisms such as congestion pricing to make more efficient use of existing infrastructure, applying updated grant design features such as varying matching requirements and maintenance of effort provisions, supporting improved data collection, and promoting intermodal approaches. Finally, bringing revenues and expenditures into balance would ensure the fiscal sustainability of surface transportation programs. The current challenge for Congress is to structure a program responsive to these 21st century principles. With the clear unsustainability and performance issues of the current program, it is an opportune time for Congress to better define the federal role in transportation and improve the progress toward specific, nationally-defined outcomes. Reforming the current approach to transportation problems will take time and it may be necessary to shift policies and programs incrementally or on a pilot basis, but a transformation of policies and programs is needed to effectively address the nation's transportation needs and priorities.

To improve the effectiveness of the federal investment in surface transportation, meet the nation's transportation needs, and ensure a sustainable commitment to transportation infrastructure, Congress should consider reexamining and refocusing surface transportation programs to be responsive to these principles so that they: (1) have well-defined goals with direct links to an identified federal interest and federal role, (2) institute processes to make grantees more accountable by establishing more performance-based links between funding and program outcomes, (3) institute tools and approaches that emphasize the return on the federal investment, and (4) address the current imbalance between federal surface transportation revenues and spending.

We provided copies of a draft of this report to DOT for its review and comment. In an e-mail on February 22, 2008, DOT noted that surface transportation programs could benefit from restructured approaches that apply data driven performance oriented criteria to enable the nation to better focus its resources on key surface transportation issues. DOT officials generally agreed with the information in this report, and they provided technical clarifications which we incorporated, as appropriate.

BACKGROUND

Since 1796, the federal government has had a role in developing and funding surface transportation infrastructure such as roads and canals to promote the nation's economic vitality and improve the quality of life for its citizens. In 1956, Congress substantially broadened the federal role in road construction by establishing the Highway Trust Fund, a dedicated source of federal revenue, to finance a national network of standardized highways, known as the Interstate Highway System. This system, financed and built in partnership with state and local government over 50 years, has become central to transportation in the United States.

Currently most federal surface transportation programs funded by the HTF span four major areas of federal investment: highway infrastructure, transit infrastructure and operations, highway safety, and motor carrier safety. Federal surface transportation funds are distributed either by a formula or on a discretionary basis through several individual grant programs.[2] These grant programs are organized by mode and administered by four of DOT's operating administrations—the Federal Highway Administration (FHWA), the Federal Transit Administration (FTA), the National Highway Traffic Safety Administration (NHTSA), and the Federal Motor Carrier Safety Administration (FMCSA).[3] The modal administrations work in partnership with the states and other grant recipients to administer federal surface transportation programs. For example the federal government currently provides financial assistance, policy direction, technical expertise and some oversight, while state and local governments are ultimately responsible for executing transportation programs by matching and distributing federal funds and by planning, selecting and supervising infrastructure projects and safety programs while complying with federal requirements. Appendix II provides further information on the current and historical operation of these federal surface transportation programs. Additionally, the federal government provides financial assistance for other surface transportation programs such as intercity passenger rail, which has received over $30 billion of federal support since its inception in 1971. However this program is financed and operated separately from other surface transportation programs and an in-depth discussion of federal intercity passenger rail assistance is not included in this report.[4]

Increases over the past 10 years in transportation spending at all levels of government have improved the physical condition of highways and transit facilities to some extent, but congestion has worsened and safety gains have leveled off. According to the most recent DOT data, between 1997 and 2004 total highway spending per year by federal, state, and local governments grew by 22.7 percent in constant dollars. During this time, DOT reported some overall improvements in physical condition for road systems and bridges. For example, the percentage of vehicle miles traveled per year on "good" pavement conditions increased from 39.4 percent to 44.2 percent and the percentage of deficient bridges fell from 29.6 percent in 1998 to 26.7 percent per year in 2004. At the same time, incidents such as the Minneapolis bridge collapse in August 2007 indicate that significant challenges remain. Furthermore, despite increases in investment levels and some improvements in physical condition, operational performance has declined. For example, during the same period the average daily duration of travel in congested conditions increased from 6.2 hours to 6.6 hours, and the extent and severity of congestion across urbanized areas also grew.[5] Transportation safety has improved considerably over the past 40 years, and although motor vehicle and large truck fatality rates have generally continued to fall modestly since the mid-1990s, the improvements yielding the greatest safety benefits (e.g., vehicle crashworthiness requirements and increases in safety belt use) have already occurred, making future progress more difficult.

Furthermore, demand on transportation facilities nationwide has grown considerably since our transportation systems were built and is projected to increase in the coming decades as population, income levels, and economic activity continue to rise. According to the Transportation Research Board, an expected population growth of 100 million people could double the demand for passenger travel by 2040.[6] Similarly, freight traffic is expected to climb by 92 percent from 2002 to 2035. These trends have the potential to substantially deepen the strain on the existing system, increasing congestion, and decreasing the reliability of our transportation network—with potentially severe consequences ranging from the economic impact of wasted time and fuel to the environmental and health concerns associated with increased fuel emissions.

Moreover, at the current fuel tax rate, revenues to support the HTF may not be sufficient to sustain it. Currently, trust fund receipts are growing and will continue to grow with increased traffic. However, the purchasing power of the dollar has declined with inflation, and the federal motor fuel tax rate has not increased since 1993. In addition, more fuel-efficient and alternative-fuel vehicles are using less taxable motor fuel per mile driven. Recent legislation has authorized spending that is expected to outstrip the growth in trust fund receipts. According to a recent estimate from CBO, the remaining balance in the Highway Account of the Highway Trust Fund[7] will be exhausted in 2009, and in fiscal year 2009 projected highway spending will exceed revenue by $4 to $5 billion.[8]

In January 2008 the National Surface Transportation Policy and Revenue Study Commission released a report with several recommendations to place the trust fund on a sustainable path, as well as reform the current structure of the nation's surface transportation programs.[9] The recommendations include significantly increasing the level of investment by all levels of the government in surface transportation, consolidating and reorganizing the current programs, speeding project delivery, and making the current program more performance- and outcome-based and mode-neutral, among other things. To finance the additional investment, the Commission recommended raising the current federal fuel tax rate by 25 to 40 cents per gallon on an incremental basis equivalent to an increase of 5 to 8 cents per gallon per year for 5 years. It also said that states would have to raise revenue from a combination of higher fuel taxes and other sources. In addition to raising the fuel tax, the Commission recommended a number of other user-based fees such as tolling, congestion pricing, and freight fees to provide additional revenue for transportation improvements.

Three members of the Commission disagreed with some of the findings and recommendations of the Commission report. For example, the minority view disagreed with the Commission's recommendations on expanding the federal role and increasing the federal fuel tax, among others. Rather, the minority view proposed sustaining fuel taxes at the current levels, refocusing federal investment on two areas of national interest, and providing the states with greater regulatory flexibility, incentives, and the analytical tools to allow adoption of market-based reforms on their highway systems. We have ongoing work assessing the Commission's proposal and other reauthorization proposals and will be issuing a report in 2008.

THE FEDERAL ROLE IN SURFACE TRANSPORTATION HAS EXPANDED TO INCLUDE BROADER GOALS, MORE PROGRAMS, AND A VARIETY OF PROGRAM STRUCTURES

Although most surface transportation funds are still directed to highway infrastructure, the federal role in surface transportation has broadened over the past 50 years to incorporate goals beyond highway construction, and federal surface transportation programs have grown in number and complexity. The resulting conglomeration of program structures reflects a variety of federal approaches for setting priorities, distributing federal funds, and sharing oversight responsibility with state and local partners for surface transportation programs.

Federal Goals Have Broadened, and Programs Have Grown in Number and Complexity

The HTF was established in 1956 to provide federal funding for Interstate highway construction and other infrastructure improvements based on the "user-pay principle"— that is, users of transportation systems should pay for the systems' construction through highway user fees such as taxes on motor fuels, tires, and trucks. However, since 1956, the federal role in surface transportation has expanded beyond funding Interstate construction and highway infrastructure to include grant programs that address other transportation, societal, and environmental goals. For example, although most HTF expenditures continue to support highway infrastructure improvements (see Figure 1), Congress established new federal grants for highway safety and transit during the 1960s and added a motor carrier safety grant program during the 1980s.[10]

Furthermore, Congress has since expanded the initial basic grant programs in each of these areas to incorporate a variety of different goals. For example, the highway program has expanded to include additional programs to fund air quality improvements, Interstate maintenance, and safety-related construction improvements (see Figure 2).

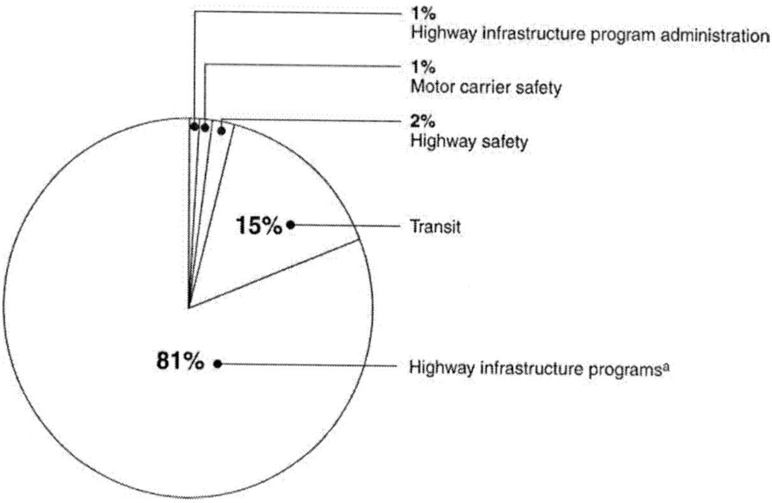

Source: GAO analysis of CBO and DOT data.

Note: Program administration costs are included in the totals for NHTSA and FMCSA. FTA program administration costs are funded by general funds.

[a] Highway infrastructure programs include highway infrastructure-related safety expenditures.

Figure 1. Budget Authority for Highway Trust Fund Expenditures by Program Area, 2007.

Federal transit assistance expanded from a single grant program that funded capital projects to multiple programs that provide general capital and operating assistance for urban and rural areas,[11] as well as numerous specialized grants with goals ranging from supporting transit service for the elderly, persons with disabilities, and low-income workers to promoting the use of alternative fuels (see Figure 3).

Federal safety assistance has also expanded from funding general state highway and motor carrier safety programs and enforcement activities to additionally funding many specialized grants to address specific issues. For example, federal highway safety assistance currently includes several grant programs to address specific accident factors (e.g., alcohol-impaired driving) and safety data gaps (see Figure 4). Similarly, the number of federal motor carrier assistance programs has increased to include several grants for improving data collection, supporting commercial driver's license programs and funding border enforcement activities (see Figure 5). Consequently, federal funds currently support a wide variety of goals and modes beyond the initial federal focus on highway infrastructure, ranging from broad support for transit in urban areas, to targeted grants to increase seat-belt usage.

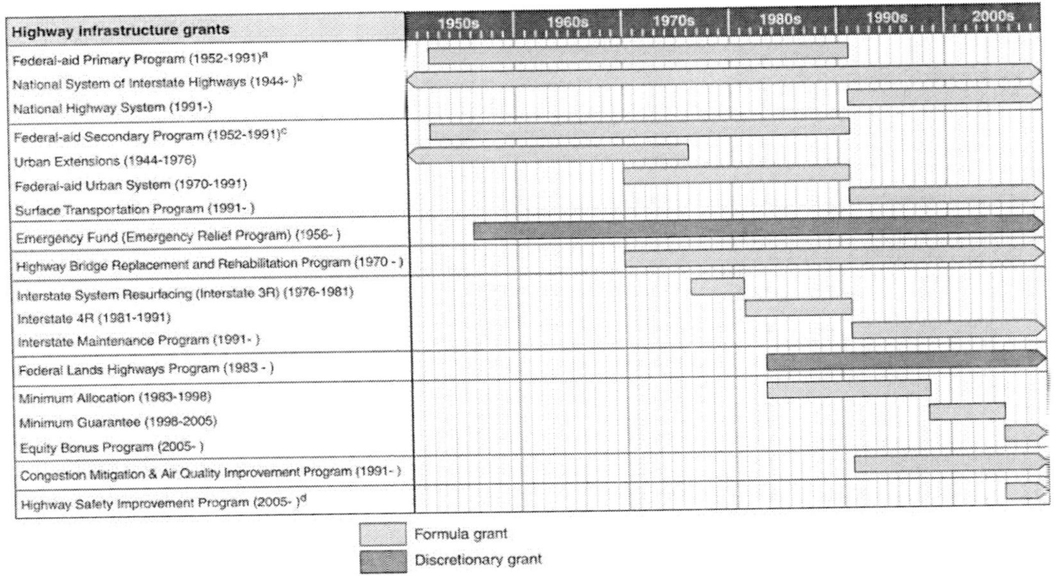

Source: GAO analysis of DOT data.Formula grantDiscretionary grant

Notes: This chart includes only a portion of federal highway infrastructure grants. As part of its report, the National Surface Transportation Policy and Revenue Study Commission identified 62 highway programs. Unless otherwise noted, start dates in the chart indicate program authorization dates. Programs that are related in purpose to grant programs in successive reauthorization legislation are included in the same row.

[a] Federal funding for primary roads was first authorized in 1921, but the separate grant program was not established until 1952.

[b] Federal funding for the Interstate Highway System was first authorized in 1944, but the separate grant program was not established until 1952. Significant funding was not provided until 1956.

[c] Federal funding for secondary roads was first authorized in 1921, but the separate grant program was not established until 1952.

[d] Prior to the establishment of the Highway Safety Improvement Program, dedicated funds for highway infrastructure-related safety expenditures were available as a set-aside under the Surface Transportation Program.

Figure 2. Historical Expansion of Major Federally Funded Highway Infrastructure Grant Programs.

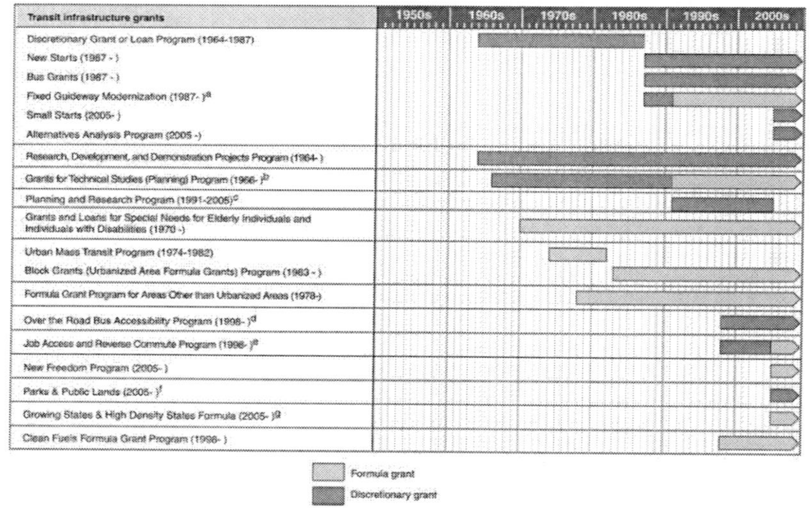

Source: GAO analysis of DOT data.

Notes: This chart includes only a portion of federal transit infrastructure grants. As part of its report, the National Surface Transportation Policy and Revenue Study Commission identified 20 transit programs. Unless otherwise noted, start dates in the chart indicate program authorization dates. Programs that are related in purpose to grant programs in successive reauthorization legislation are included in the same row.

[a] In 1991, Fixed Guideway Modernization changed from a discretionary grant to a formula grant program.

[b] In 1991, Grants for Technical Studies Program changed from a discretionary grant to a formula grant program. This program currently funds both state and local planning activities.

[c] Planning and Research Program provided separate funding to states for planning and research activities. Research funds were distributed on a discretionary basis and planning funds were distributed on a formula basis.

[d] Over the Road Bus Accessibility Program is also referred to as the Rural Transportation Accessibility Incentive Program. Page 14 GAO-08-400

[e] In 2005, Job Access and Reverse Commute Program changed from a discretionary grant to a formula grant program.

[f] Parks and Public Lands is also referred to as Alternative Transportation in Parks and Public Land.

[g] Growing States and High Density States Formula is also referred to as Apportionments Based on Growing States Formula Factors.

Figure 3. Historical Expansion of Major Federally Funded Transit Infrastructure Programs.

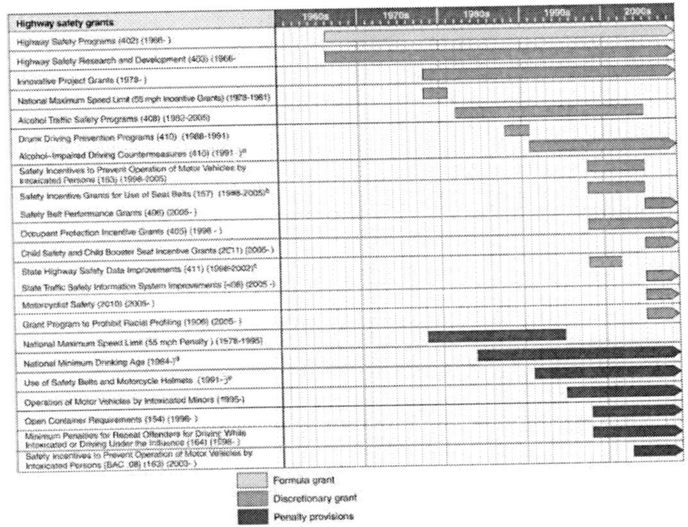

Source: GAO analysis of DOT data.Formula grantDiscretionary grantPenalty provisions

Notes: This chart includes only a portion of federal highway safety and motor carrier safety grants. As part of its report, the National Surface Transportation Policy and Revenue Study Commission identified 12 highway safety grant programs. Unless otherwise noted, start dates in the chart indicate program authorization dates. Programs that are related in purpose to grant programs in successive reauthorization legislation are included in the same row.

[a] Alcohol-Impaired Driving Countermeasures was funded out of Highway Safety Programs Section 402 funds from 1993–1997.

[b] Safety Incentive Grants for Use of Seat Belts remains authorized but has not been funded since 2005.

[c] State Highway Safety Data Improvements remains authorized but has not been funded since 2002, when the program funds were fully disbursed

[d] National Minimum Drinking Age penalty provisions were authorized in 1984, but did not take effect until 1987.

[e] The motorcycle helmet penalty provision of Use of Safety Belts and Motorcycle Helmets was repealed in 1995.

Figure 4. Historical Expansion of Major Federally Funded Highway Safety Programs.

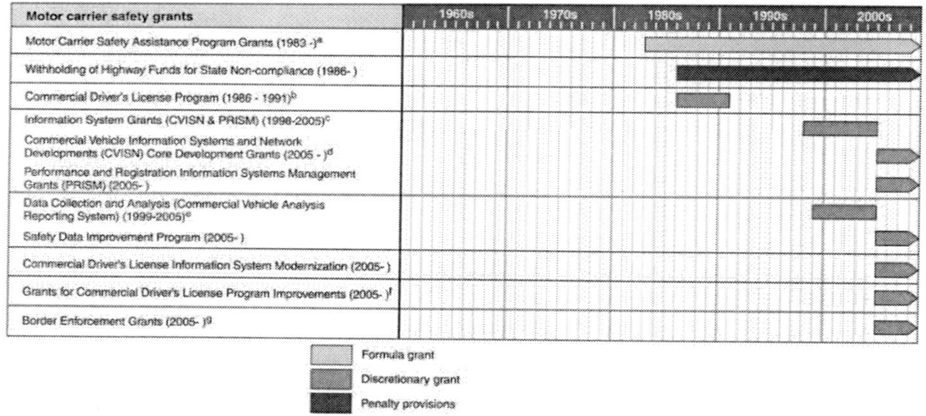

Source: GAO analysis of DOT data.

Notes: This chart includes only a portion of motor carrier safety grants. Smaller grant programs such as the Grant Program for Commercial Motor Vehicle Operators were not included. Unless otherwise noted, start dates in the chart indicate program authorization dates. Programs that are related in purpose to grant programs in successive reauthorization legislation are included in the same row.

[a] Formula basis for distributing funds was established by the agency rather than by statute.

[b] Commercial Driver's License Program (CDLP) funding began in 1987 and was provided by four separate grants in the authorizing legislation. The program name was not established by statute but DOT refers to the program as CDLP.

[c] Information System Grants remains authorized, but has not been funded since 2005.

[d] CVISN Deployment activities were also funded from 1998–2005 as part of DOT's Intelligent Transportation Systems (ITS) Deployment Program, and from 1994–1998 through the Intelligent Vehicle Highway System Program.

[e] Data Collection and Analysis program was jointly administered with NHTSA. In 2005, the program was reauthorized as the Safety Data Improvement Program.

[f] FMCSA provided funds to states for commercial drivers license programs on an emergency basis from 2001–2003.

[g] Although authorized in 2005, Border Enforcement Grants program did not distribute funds until 2006. FMCSA also funded border enforcement activities from other sources during 2004 and 2005.

Figure 5.Historical Expansion of Major Federally Funded Motor Carrier Safety Programs.

Furthermore, Congress has also expanded the scope of federal safety goals to include specific legislative changes at the state level. For example, in accepting certain federal-aid highway infrastructure funds, states must enact certain laws to improve highway safety or face penalties in the form of either withholdings or transfers in their federal grants. Over the past 30 years, penalty or incentive provisions have been used to encourage states to enact laws that establish a minimum drinking age of 21 years, a maximum blood alcohol level of 0.08 to determine impaired driving ability, and mandatory seat belt usage, among others (see Figure 4), with transfer or withholding penalties as high as 10 percent of a state's designated highway infrastructure funds. While most states have chosen to adopt laws that comply with many of these provisions, some remain subject to certain penalties. For example, as of January 2008, 11 states are penalized for not enacting an open container law and 11 are penalized for not enacting a repeat offender law.

As federal goals have broadened, Congress has added new federal procedural requirements for infrastructure projects and programs and agencies have issued more complex rules to address these additional federal goals. For example, Congress established cooperative urban transportation planning as a matter of national interest and passed legislation in 1962 requiring all construction projects to be part of a continuing, comprehensive, and cooperative planning process between state and local governments.[12] In another example, grant recipients may be required to conduct environmental assessments for many federally funded transportation projects to comply with the federal environmental goals established by the National Environmental Policy Act of 1969 (NEPA).[13] Other federal requirements may include compliance with the Americans with Disabilities Act, nondiscrimination clauses in the Civil Rights Act of 1964, labor standards mandated by the Davis-Bacon Act, and Buy America procurement provisions, among others.

Although behavior-oriented safety programs and activities are generally not subject to construction-related requirements, Congress has required that agencies address additional federal goals in safety-related rulemaking processes. For example, to address national environmental objectives, Congress expanded NHTSA's regulatory scope in highway safety to include establishing regulations for corporate average fuel economy standards, in addition to issuing rules in areas such as tire-safety standards and occupant-protection devices (e.g., seat belts). Similarly, to address other areas of national concern, Congress has broadened FMCSA's regulatory authority in motor carrier safety to include household goods movement, medical requirements for motor carrier operators, and greater oversight of border and international safety.[14] Furthermore, when establishing federal standards in these areas, regulatory agencies such as NHTSA and FMCSA may be subject to increasingly rigorous requirements for analysis and justification associated with a wide range of federal legislation and executive orders including NEPA, Executive Order 12866 requiring cost-benefit analysis for proposed rules,[15] Executive Order 13211 requiring consideration of the effects of government regulation on energy, and the Unfunded Mandates Reform Act of 1995, among others.

Current Program Structures Reflect a Variety of Federal Approaches to Surface Transportation

Program expansion over the past 50 years has created a variety of grant structures and established different federal approaches for setting priorities and distributing federal funds across surface transportation programs. These approaches, which range from formula grants to dedicated spending provisions, give state and local governments varying degrees of discretion in allocating federal funds. As in the past, most surface transportation programs are jointly administered by the federal government in partnership with state or local governments, but in recent years the federal government has increasingly delegated oversight responsibility to state and local governments.

Federal Responsibility for Establishing Priorities and Directing Funds Varies across Programs

Federal approaches for setting priorities and distributing funds currently range from giving state and local governments broad discretion in allocating highway infrastructure funds to directly targeting specific federal goals through the use of incentive grants and penalty provisions in safety programs. In 1956 federal surface transportation funds were distributed to the states through four formula grant programs that provided federal construction aid for certain eligible highway categories (e.g., Interstate, primary, and secondary highways and urban extensions). The states in turn, matched and distributed funds at their discretion, within each program's eligibility requirements. Within the highway program, this federal-state partnership has changed in response to considerable increases in state and local authority and flexibility since 1956.

Largely because of revisions to federal highway programs in the 1990s, state and local governments currently have greater discretion to allocate the majority of their federal highway funds according to state and local priorities. For example, core highway programs such as the Surface Transportation Program and the National Highway System program have broader goals and project eligibility requirements than earlier highway infrastructure grant programs.[16] Although funds continue to be distributed by formula to the states for individual programs based on measures of highway use or the extent of a state's highway network, or other factors, as figure 6 demonstrates, six core highway programs permit the states to transfer up to 50 percent of their apportioned funds, with certain restrictions, to other eligible highway programs. Furthermore, although the process for calculating the distributions is complex for some programs, the end result of most highway program formulas is heavily influenced by minimum apportionment[17] and "equity" requirements. For fiscal year 2008, each state's share of formula funds will be at least 92 percent of their relative revenue contributions to the Highway Account of the Highway Trust Fund.[18] According to FHWA estimates, the equity requirements will provide approximately $9 billion in highway funds to the states in addition to the amount distributed by formula through the individual grant programs.[19] Over $2 billion of these additional funds will have the same broad eligibility requirements and transfer provisions of the Surface Transportation Program. Moreover, flexible funding provisions within highway and transit programs allow certain infrastructure funds to be used interchangeably for highway or transit projects.

Major transit infrastructure grants currently range from broad formula grants that provide capital and operating assistance,[20] such as the Block Grants Program (Urbanized Area Formula Grants), to targeted discretionary grants for new transit systems, such as New Starts and Small Starts, that require applicants to compete for funding based on statutorily defined criteria. For example, projects must compete for New Starts funds on the basis of cost-effectiveness, potential mobility improvements, environmental benefits, and economic development effects, among other factors.[21] Additionally, smaller formula grants direct funds to general goals such as supporting transit services for special populations like elderly, disabled, and low-income persons. Unlike most surface transportation funding, which is distributed through the states, most transit assistance is distributed directly to local agencies, since transit assistance was originally focused on urban areas.

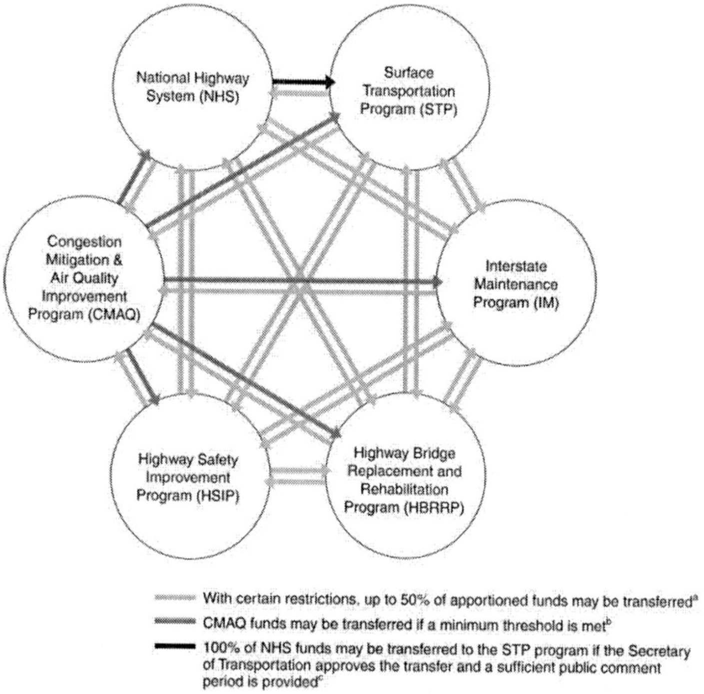

Source: GAO.

[a] TEA-21, Pub. L. No. 105-178 §1310, (June 9, 1998), codified at 23 USC §126(a).

[b] Ibid.

[c] 23 USC §104.

Figure 6. Broad Flexible Fund Transfer Provisions within Highway Programs.

Current major highway and motor carrier safety grants include formula grants to provide general assistance for state highway safety programs and improving motor carrier safety and enforcement activities, such as Highway Safety Programs (402) and Motor Carrier Safety Assistance Program (MCSAP) Grants. They also include targeted discretionary grants such as Occupant Protection Incentive Grants and Border Enforcement Grants. Additionally, they include penalty provisions, such as Open Container Requirements (154) and Minimum Penalties for Repeat Offenders for Driving While Intoxicated or Driving Under the Influence (164), designed to address specific safety areas of national interest. Unlike formula-based funding, some of the discretionary grants, such as the Safety Belt Performance Grants, directly promote national priorities by providing financial incentives for meeting specific performance or safety activity criteria (e.g., enforcement, outreach). Additionally, penalty provisions such as those associated with Open Container laws and MCSAP Grants promote federal priorities by either transferring or withholding state highway infrastructure funds from states that do not comply with certain federal provisions. For example, in 2007, penalty provisions transferred over $217 million of federal highway infrastructure assistance to highway safety programs in the 19 states and Puerto Rico that were penalized for failure to enact either open container or repeat offender laws.

Finally, Congress provides congressionally directed spending for surface transportation through specific provisions in legislation or committee reports. While estimates of the precise number and value of these congressional directives vary, observers agree that they have grown dramatically. For instance, the Transportation Research Board found that congressional directives have grown from 11 projects in the 1982 reauthorization act to over 5,000 projects in the 2005 reauthorization act.[22]

State and Local Government Oversight Responsibilities Have Increased

Most federal surface transportation programs continue to be jointly administered by the federal and state, or local governments, but the federal government has increasingly delegated oversight responsibility to state and local governments. This trend is most pronounced for highway infrastructure programs; however, it has also occurred in federal transit and safety programs. For example, when Interstate construction began, the federal government fully oversaw all federally funded construction projects, including approving design plans, specifications, and estimates, and periodically inspecting construction progress. In 1973, Congress authorized DOT to delegate oversight responsibility to states for compliance with certain federal requirements for noninterstate projects.[23] During the 1990s, Congress further expanded this authority to allow states and FHWA to cooperatively determine the appropriate level of oversight for federally funded projects, including some Interstate projects.[24] Currently, based on a stewardship agreement with each state, FHWA exercises full oversight over a limited number Federal-aid Highway projects, constituting a relatively limited amount of highway mileage. States are required to oversee all Federal-aid Highway projects that are not on the National Highway System, which constitutes a large majority of the road mileage receiving federal funds, and states oversee design and construction phases of other projects based on an agreement between FHWA and the state. Full federal oversight for transit projects is limited to major capital projects that cost over $100 million, and grant recipients are allowed to self-certify their compliance with certain federal laws and regulations for other projects. Although state and local grant recipients have considerable oversight authority, FHWA and FTA both periodically review the recipients' program management processes to ensure compliance with federal laws and regulations.

State and local government responsibilities for overseeing transportation planning processes have also grown in recent decades. Although such responsibilities predate federal transportation assistance programs, since 1962, the federal government has made compliance with numerous planning and project selection requirements a condition for receiving federal assistance.[25] During the 1970s, federal requirements grew in range and complexity and, in some cases, specified how state and local governments should conduct planning activities. However, since the 1980s, state and local governments have had greater flexibility to fulfill federal planning requirements. For example, in 1983, urban transportation planning regulations were revised to reduce the level of direct federal involvement in state and local planning processes, and state and local agencies were allowed to self-certify their compliance with federal planning requirements. Similarly, although the federal government identified specific environmental and economic factors to be considered in the planning process as part of the surface transportation program legislation enacted in 1991 and subsequently amended in 1998, these requirements give state and local governments considerable discretion in selecting analytical tools to evaluate projects and make investment decisions based on their communities' needs and priorities.

The states have also been given greater oversight responsibility for safety programs as federal agencies have shifted from direct program oversight to performance-based oversight of state safety goals. For example, since 1998, NHTSA has not approved state highway safety plans or projects, but instead focuses on a state's progress in achieving the goals it set for itself in its annual safety performance plan. Under this arrangement, a state must provide an annual report that outlines the state's progress towards meeting its goals and performance measures and the contribution of funded projects toward meeting its goals. If a state does not meet its established safety goals, NHTSA and the state work cooperatively to create a safety improvement plan. FMCSA uses a similar approach to oversee state motor carrier safety activities. Starting in 1997, the states were required to identify motor carrier safety problems based on safety data analysis, target their grant activities to address these issues, and report on their progress toward the national goal of reducing truck crashes, injuries, and fatalities. Much as FHWA and FTA do for their grant programs, both NHTSA and FMCSA periodically review state management processes for compliance with federal laws and regulations.

CURRENT FEDERAL SURFACE TRANSPORTATION PROGRAMS DO NOT EFFECTIVELY ADDRESS IDENTIFIED TRANSPORTATION CHALLENGES

Many federal surface transportation programs do not effectively address identified transportation challenges such as growing congestion. While program goals are numerous, they are sometimes conflicting and often unclear—which contributes to a corresponding lack of clarity in the federal role. The largest highway, transit, and safety grant programs distribute funds through formulas that are typically not linked to performance and, in many cases, have only an indirect relationship to needs. Mechanisms generally do not link programs to the federal objectives they are intended to address, in part due to the wide discretion granted to states and localities in using most federal funds. Furthermore, surface transportation programs often do not employ the best tools and approaches available, such as rigorous economic analysis for project selection and a mode-neutral approach to planning and investment.

There Is No Clear, Consistent Federal Role in Surface Transportation

The federal role in surface transportation is unclear, in part because program goals are often unclear. In some cases, stated goals may be contradictory or may come into direct conflict.[26] For example, it may not be possible to improve air quality while spurring economic development with new highway construction. With the proliferation of goals and programs discussed in the previous section of this report, the federal role varies from funding improvements in specific types of infrastructure (such as the National Highway System) to aiming at specific outcomes (such as reducing highway fatalities). At a recent expert panel on transportation policy convened by the Comptroller General, experts cited the lack of focus of the federal role in transportation as a problem, and some stakeholders have also made similar criticisms.

In some policy areas, the federal role is limited despite consensus on goals. For example, freight movement is widely viewed as a top priority, yet no clear federal role has been established in freight policy. DOT's draft *Framework for a National Freight Policy*, issued in 2006, is a step toward clarifying a federal role and strategy, but it lacks specific targets and strategies and criteria for achieving them.[27] Current approaches to planning and financing transportation infrastructure do not effectively address freight transportation issues—few programs are directly aimed at freight movement, and funding is based on individual modes, but freight moves across many modes.[28] Similarly, despite statutes and regulations that identify an intermodal approach that provides connections across modes as a goal of federal transportation policy, there is currently only one federal program[29] specifically designed for intermodal infrastructure, and all the funds available for the program are congressionally designated for specific projects.[30]

The federal government also lacks a defined role in or mechanism for aiding projects that span multiple jurisdictions.[31] The discretion and differing priorities of individual states and localities can make it difficult to coordinate large projects that involve more than one state or local sponsor.[32] There have been some successful multijurisdictional transportation initiatives, such as the FAST Corridor across several metropolitan areas in Washington State,[33] but a lack of established political or administrative mechanisms for cooperation, combined with the large degree of state and local autonomy in transportation decision-making, is an obstacle to such "megaprojects."[34] At a hearing of the National Surface Transportation Policy and Revenue Study Commission in New York City, an expert on the regional economy cited the Tappan Zee Bridge in New York State as an example of the obstacles such projects can face. Neighboring Connecticut wants the bridge's capacity expanded, but there is currently no established mechanism that allows Connecticut to help move the project forward.[35] In testimony for the Commission, stakeholders such as the U.S. Chamber of Commerce and the American Association of Port Authorities cited fostering interjurisdictional coordination as a key federal role, and AASHTO has also highlighted the need for improved multijurisdictional coordination mechanisms in its reports on the future of federal transportation policy.[36]

At times, DOT has undertaken new activities without assessing the rationale for a federal role. For example, the agency made short sea shipping[37] of freight a priority, but did not first examine the effect of federal involvement on the industry or identify obstacles to success and potential mitigating actions. Without a consistent approach to identifying the rationale for a federal role, DOT is limited in its ability to evaluate potential investments and determine whether short sea shipping—or another available measure—is the most effective means of enhancing freight mobility.[38]

Most Programs Do Not Link Funding to Performance and Lack Mechanisms to Ensure That Stated Objectives Are Met

Most federal surface transportation programs lack links between funding and performance.[39] Federal funding for transportation has increased significantly in recent years, but because spending is not explicitly linked to performance, it is difficult to assess the impact of these increases on the achievement of key goals. During this period of funding increases, the physical condition of the highway system has improved, but the system's overall performance has decreased, according to available measures of congestion.[40] DOT has established goals under the Government Performance and Results Act (GPRA) of 1993 that set specific benchmarks for performance outcomes such as congestion and highway fatalities. However, these performance measures are not well-reflected in individual grant programs because disbursements are seldom linked to outcomes—most highway funds are apportioned without relationship to the performance of the recipients. The largest transit and safety programs also lack links to performance.[41] States and localities receive the same disbursement regardless of their performance at, for example, reducing congestion or managing project costs. As a result, the incentive to improve return on investment—the public benefits gained from public resources expended—is reduced.

Safety and some transit grants are more directly linked to goals than highway infrastructure programs, and several incorporate performance measures. Whereas highway infrastructure programs tend to focus on improving specific types of facilities such as bridges, highway safety, and, to a lesser extent, transit programs, are more often designed to achieve specific objectives. For instance, the goal of the Job Access and Reverse Commute transit program is to make jobs more accessible for welfare recipients and other low-income individuals. Likewise, under the Section 402 State and Community Highway Safety Grant Program, funds must be used to further the goal of reducing highway fatalities.[42] To some extent, transit and safety programs also have a more direct link to needs because their formulas do not incorporate equity adjustments that seek to return funds to their source. Furthermore, several highway safety and motor carrier safety grants make use of performance measures and incentives. For example, under the Motor Carrier Safety Assistance Program, some funds are set aside for incentive grants that are awarded using five state performance indicators that include, among others, large truck-involved vehicle fatality rates, data sharing, and commercial driver's license verification.[43]

Most highway transportation programs lack links to need as well as performance. As discussed above, most grant funds are instead distributed according to set formulas that typically have an indirect relation to need. As a result, grant disbursements for these programs not only fail to reflect performance, but they may also not reflect need.[44] Some of the formula criteria, such as population, are indirect measures of need, but the equity bonus[45] and minimum apportionment criteria are not related to need, and exert a strong influence on formula outcomes. Certain programs, such as the Highway Bridge Replacement and Rehabilitation Program, which bases disbursements on the cost of needed repairs, use more direct measures.[46] In general, however, the link between needs and federal highway funding is weak.

Besides lacking links between funding and performance, federal surface transportation programs generally lack mechanisms to tie state actions to program goals. DOT does not have direct control over the vast majority of activities that it funds; instead, states and localities have wide discretion in selecting projects to fund with federal grants.[47] Federal law calls the federal-aid highway program a "federally-assisted state program," and specifies that grant funds "shall in no way infringe on the sovereign rights of the States to determine which projects shall be federally financed."[48] In addition, states have broad flexibility in using more than half of federal highway funds as a result of a combination of programs with wide eligibility (such as the Surface Transportation Program) and the ability to transfer some funds between highway programs.[49] Furthermore, "flex funding" provisions allow transfers between eligible highway and transit programs; between 1992 and 2006, states used this authority to transfer $12 billion from highway to transit programs.[50] While these provisions give states the discretion to pursue their own priorities, the provisions may impede the targeting of federal funds toward specific national objectives. Federal rules for transferring funds between highway programs are so flexible that the distinctions between individual programs have little meaning. To some extent, the Federal-aid Highway program functions as a cash transfer, general purpose grant program, not as a tool for pursuing a cohesive national transportation policy.[51] Transit and safety grants, in contrast, are more linked to goals because they do not allow transfers among programs to the same degree.[52] Safety grants are linked to goals because states must use data on safety measures to create performance plans that structure their safety investments, yet states are still able to set their own goals, develop their own programs, and select their own projects. Performance measures are also used in allocating funding in several highway safety grant programs, providing an even more direct link to goals.[53]

Programs Do Not Employ the Best Tools and Approaches to Ensure Effective Investment Decisions

In some areas, federal surface transportation programs do not use the best tools and approaches available. Rigorous economic analysis, applied in benefit-cost studies, is a key tool for targeting investments, but does not drive transportation decision-making. While such analysis is sometimes used, we have previously reported that it is generally only a small factor in a given investment decision.[54] Furthermore, statutory requirements of the planning and project selection processes—such as public participation procedures or NEPA requirements that may be difficult to translate into economic terms—can interfere with the use of benefit-cost analysis. Decision makers often also see other factors as more important. In a survey of state DOTs that we conducted in 2004 as part of that same study, 34 said that political support and public opinion are factors of great or very great importance in the decision to recommend a highway project, while 8 said that the ratio of benefits to costs was a factor of great or very great importance. Economic analysis was more common for transit projects, largely because of the requirements of the competitive New Starts grant program, which uses a cost-effectiveness measure. However, the New Starts program constitutes only 18 percent of transit funding authorizations under the Safe, Accountable, Flexible, and Efficient Transportation Equity Act – A Legacy for Users (SAFETEA-LU) authorization.[55] There are also few formal evaluations of the outcomes of federally-funded projects. As a result, policymakers miss a chance to learn more about the efficacy of different approaches and projects. Such evaluations are especially important because highway and transit projects often have higher costs and lower usage than estimated beforehand.[56] New Starts is also the only transportation grant program that requires before-and-after studies of outcomes.[57]

The modal basis of transportation funding also limits opportunities to invest scarce resources as efficiently as possible. Instead of being linked to desired outcomes, such as mobility improvements, funds are "stovepiped" by transportation mode.[58] Although, as discussed above, states and localities have great flexibility in how they use their funds, this modal structure can still discourage investments based on an intermodal approach and cross-modal comparisons.[59] Reflecting the separate federal transportation funding programs, many state and local DOTs are organized into several operating administrations with responsibilities for particular modes. Because different operating administrations oversee and manage separate funding programs, these programs often have differing timelines, criteria, and matching fund requirements, which can make it difficult for public planners to pursue the goal—stated in law and DOT policy—of an intermodal approach to transportation needs. For example, a recent project at the Port of Tacoma (Washington) involved widening a road and relocating rail tracks to improve freight movement on both modes, but it was delayed because highway funding was available, but rail funding was not. Moreover, despite the wide funding flexibility within the highway program and between the highway and transit programs, many funds are dedicated on a modal basis, and state and local decision makers may choose projects based on the mode eligible for federal funding.[60] Experts on the Comptroller General's recent transportation policy panel cited modal stovepiping as a problem with the current federal structure, saying that it inhibits consideration of a range of transportation options.[61] State officials have also criticized stovepiping, both in AASHTO policy statements and individually.[62] For instance, a state transportation official told a hearing of the National Surface Transportation Policy and Revenue Study Commission that modal flexibility should be increased to allow states to select the best project to address a given goal.[63]

The federal government is not equipped to implement a performance-based approach to transportation funding in many areas because it lacks comprehensive data. Data on outcomes—ideally covering all projects and parts of the national transportation network, as well as all modes—would be needed in order to consider performance in funding decisions. Presently, data on key performance and outcome indicators is often absent or flawed. For example, DOT does not have a central source of data on congestion—the available data are stovepiped by mode—and some congestion information for freight rail is inaccessible because it is proprietary and controlled by railroad companies.[64] Likewise, FTA does not possess reliable and complete data on transit safety.[65] A partial exception is highway safety, for which NHTSA and FMCSA have data on a variety of outcomes, such as traffic fatalities. NHTSA employs this information to help states set priorities, FMCSA uses it to target enforcement activities, and both agencies use it to monitor states' progress toward achieving their goals and to award incentive grants. However, the safety data that states collect are not always timely, complete, and consistent. For example, a review of selected states found that some of the information in their databases was several years old.[66]

Tools to make better use of existing infrastructure have not been deployed to their full potential, in part because their implementation is inhibited by the current structure of federal programs. Research has shown that a variety of congestion management tools, such as Intelligent Transportation Systems (ITS) and congestion pricing[67] are effective ways of increasing or better utilizing capacity.[68] Although such tools are increasingly employed by states and localities, their adoption has not been as extensive as it could be given their potential to decrease congestion. One factor contributing to this slow implementation is the lack of a link between funding and performance in current federal programs—projects with a lower return on investment may be funded instead of congestion management tools such as ITS. Furthermore, DOT's measures of effects fall short of capturing the impact of ITS on congestion, making it more difficult for decision makers to assess the relative worth of alternative solutions. State autonomy also contributes to the slowed rollout of these tools. Even though federal funding is available to encourage investment in ITS, states often opt for investments in more visible projects that meet public demands, such as capacity expansion.[69]

Federal investment in transportation may lead to the substitution of federal spending for state and local spending. One strategy that Congress has used to meet the goals of the Federal-aid Highway program has been to increase federal investment. However, not all of the increased federal investment has increased the total investment in highways, in part because Congress cannot prevent states and localities from using some of their own highway funds for other purposes when they receive additional federal funds. We reported, on the basis of our own modeling and a review of other empirical studies, that increased federal highway grants influence states and localities to substitute federal funds for funds they otherwise would have spent on highways.[70] Specifically, we studied the period from 1983 through 2000 and our model suggests that over the entire time period, states substituted about 50 cents of every dollar increase in federal highways grants for funds they would have spent on highways from their own resources. For the latter part of that period, 1992 through 2000, we estimated a substitution rate of about 60 cents for every dollar increase in federal aid. These results were consistent with other study findings and indicate that substitution is reducing the impact of federal investment.[71] Federal grant programs have generally not employed the best tools and approaches to reduce this potential for substitution—maintenance of effort requirements and higher nonfederal matching requirements, discussed in the next section of this report. One reason for the high rate of substitution for the Federal-aid Highway program is that states typically spend more than the amount required to meet federal matching requirements—generally 20 percent. Thus, states can reduce their own highway spending and still obtain increased federal funds.[72]

Finally, congressionally directed spending may not be an ideal means of allocating federal grant funds. Some argue that Members of Congress are good judges of investment needs in their districts, and some congressional directives are requested by states. However, officials from FHWA and FTA have stated that congressional directives sometimes displace their priority transportation projects by providing funds for projects that would not have been chosen in a competitive selection process. For example, FHWA officials stated that some congressional directives listed in the Projects of National and Regional Significance program[73] would not have qualified for funding in a merit-based selection process.[74] Officials from three state departments of transportation also noted that inflexibilities in the use of congressionally directed funds limit the states' ability to implement projects and efficiently use transportation funds by, for example, providing funding for projects that are not yet ready for implementation or providing insufficient funds to complete particular projects. However, an official from one state department of transportation noted that although congressional directives can create administrative challenges, they often represent funding that the state may not have otherwise received.

Sustainability of Transportation Financing Threatened by Funding Imbalance and Long-Term Trends

The solvency of the federal surface transportation program is at risk because expenditures now exceed revenues for the Highway Trust Fund, and projections indicate that the balance of the Highway Trust Fund will soon be exhausted. According to the Congressional Budget Office, the Highway Account will face a shortfall in 2009, the Transit Account in 2012.[75] The rate of expenditures has affected its fiscal sustainability. As a result of the Transportation Equity Act for the 21st Century (TEA-21), Highway Trust Fund spending rose 40 percent from 1999 to 2003 and averaged $36.3 billion in contract authority per year, and the upward trend in expenditures continued under SAFETEA-LU, which provided an average of $57.2 billion in contract authority per year.

Congress also established a revenue-aligned budget authority (RABA) mechanism in TEA-21 to help assure that the Highway Trust Fund would be used to fund projects instead of accumulating large balances.[76] When revenues into the Highway Trust Fund are higher than forecast, RABA ensures that additional funds are apportioned to the states. The RABA provisions were written so that the adjustments could work in either direction—going up when the trust fund had greater revenues than projected and down when revenues did not meet projected levels. However, when the possibility of a downward adjustment occurred in fiscal year 2003 as a result of lower-than-projected trust fund revenues, Congress chose to maintain spending at the fiscal year 2002 level. If the RABA approach is kept in the future, allowing downward adjustments could help with the overall sustainability of the fund.

While expenditures from the trust fund have grown, revenues into the fund have not kept pace. The current 18.4 cents per gallon fuel tax has been in place since 1993, and the buying power of the fixed cents-per-gallon amount has since been eroded by inflation. The reallocation to the Highway Trust Fund of 4.3 cents of federal fuel tax previously dedicated to deficit reduction provided an influx of funds beginning in 1997. However, this influx has been insufficient to sustain current funding levels. In addition, if changes are not made in policy to compensate for both the increased use of alternative fuels that are not currently taxed and increased fuel economy, fuel tax revenues, which still account for the majority of federal transportation financing, may further erode in the future.[77]

Principles Can Guide Assessment of Options to Restructure Federal Surface Transportation Programs

A sound basis for reexamination can productively begin with identification of and debate on underlying principles. Through our prior work on reexamining the base of government, our analysis of existing programs and other prior reports, we identified a number of principles that could help drive reexamination of federal surface transportation programs and an assessment of options for restructuring the federal surface transportation program. The appropriateness of these options will depend on the underlying federal interest and the relative potential of the options to develop sustainable strategies addressing complex national transportation challenges. These principles are as follows:

- Create well-defined goals based on identified areas of federal interest.
- Establish and clearly define the federal role in achieving each goal.
- Incorporate performance and accountability for results into funding decisions.
- Employ best tools and approaches to emphasize return on investment.
- Ensure fiscal sustainability.

Create Well-Defined Goals Based on Identified Areas of Federal Interest

Determining the federal interest involves examining the relevance and relative priority of existing programs in light of 21st century challenges and identifying emerging areas of national importance. For instance, increases in passenger and freight travel have led to growing congestion, and this strain on the transportation system is expected to grow with population increases, technology changes, and the globalization of the economy. Furthermore, experts have suggested that federal transportation policy should recognize emerging national and global imperatives such as reducing the nation's dependence on foreign fuel sources and minimizing the impact of the transportation system on global climate change. Given these and other challenges, it is important to assess the continued relevance of established federal programs and to determine whether the current areas of federal involvement are still areas of national interest. Key to such an assessment is how narrowly or broadly the federal interest in the nation's transportation system should be defined and whether the federal interest is greater in certain areas of national priority:

- Should federal spending and programs be more focused on specific national interests such as interstate freight mobility or on broad corridor development?
- Is there a federal interest in local issues such as urban congestion? If so, are there more distinct ways in which federal transportation spending and programs could address local issues that would enhance inherent local incentives and choices?

- To what extent should federal transportation policy address social concerns such as mobility for disadvantaged persons and transportation safety?
- If environmental stewardship is part of the federal interest, how might federal transportation policy better integrate national long-term goals related to energy independence and climate change?

The proliferation of federal surface transportation programs has, over time, resulted in an amalgam of policy interests that may not accurately reflect current national concerns and priorities. Although policymakers have attempted to clarify federal transportation policy in the past[78] and an FHWA Task Force has called for focusing federal involvement on activities that clearly promote national objectives, current policy statements continue to cover a wide spectrum of broadly defined federal interests ranging from promoting global competitiveness to improving citizens' quality of life. While these federal programs, activities, and funding flows reflect the interests of various constituencies, they are not as a whole aligned with a strategic, coherent, and well-defined national interest. In short, the overarching federal interest has blurred. Once the federal interest has been refocused and more clearly defined, policymakers will have a foundation for allocating scarce federal resources according to the level of national interest.

With the federal interest in surface transportation clearly defined, policymakers can clarify the goals for federal involvement. The more specific, measurable, achievable, and outcome-based the goals are, the better the foundation will be for allocating resources and optimizing results. Even though some federal transportation safety programs are linked to measurable outcome-based goals, such as achieving a specific rate of safety-belt use to reduce traffic fatalities, the formula funding for general improvements to transit facilities or highway systems is generally provided without reference to achieving specific outcomes for federal involvement. For example, the guidelines for state and local recipients' use of the largest highway and transit formula grant funds, such as the Surface Transportation Program or Block Grant Program (Urbanized Area Formula Grants), are based on broad project eligibility criteria. These criteria involve the type of highway or type of work (e.g., transit capital investment versus operating assistance) rather than the achievement of clearly defined and measurable outcomes.[79] Furthermore, although DOT has already established some outcome measures as part of its strategic planning process, its agencywide goals and outcomes cover a vast array of activities and are generally not directly linked to project selection or funding decisions for most highway funding and the largest transit and safety programs. Without specific and measurable outcomes for federal involvement, policymakers will have difficulty determining whether certain programs are achieving desired results.

Establish and Clearly Define the Federal Role in Achieving Each Goal

After identifying the federal interest and federal goals, policymakers can clearly define the federal government's role in working toward each goal and define that role in relation to the roles of other levels of government and other stakeholders. This would involve an examination of state and local government roles, as well as of the federal role. Following such an examination, the current relationship between the federal and other levels of government could change. For example, in the federal-aid highway program, the current "partnership" between the federal government and the states is based on an explicit recognition of state sovereignty in the conduct of the program, and the states have considerable flexibility in moving funds within this program. By contrast, highway safety programs operate under a grantor-grantee relationship and for transit the grantees are largely local units of government, although the role of states has grown. An examination of these programs could change these relationships, since different federal goals may require different degrees and types of federal involvement. Where the federal interest is greatest, the federal government may play a more direct role in setting priorities and allocating resources, as well as fund a higher share of program costs. Conversely, where the federal interest is less evident, state and local governments could assume more responsibility.

Functions that other entities may perform better than the federal government could be turned back to the states or other levels of government. Given the already substantial roles states and localities play in the construction and operation of transportation facilities, there may be areas that no longer call for federal involvement and funding could be reassessed. Notably, we have reported that the modal focus of federal programs can distort the investment and decision-making of other levels of government and a streamlining of federal goals and priorities could better align programs with desired outcomes. Turning functions back to the states has many other implications. For example, states would likely have to raise additional revenues to support the increased responsibilities. While states might be freer to allocate funds internally without modally stovepiped federal funding categories, some states could face legal funding restrictions. For example, some states prohibit the use of highway funds for transit purposes, so if a transit program were returned to the states, alternative taxes would have to be raised or the laws would have to be changed. Until a program or function is actually turned back to the states or localities, it is uncertain how these other levels of government will perform. For example, if highway safety programs were turned back to the states, it is not known whether states would continue to target the same issues that they currently choose to address under federally-funded programs or would emphasize different issues. Likewise, if a program that targets a specific area such as urban transit systems is turned back to the states, there is no assurance that the states would continue to fund this area. Turning programs back to the states would have far-reaching consequences, as discussed in appendix III.

Observers have argued that certain issues, such as urban mobility, are essentially metropolitan in character and therefore should be addressed by metropolitan regions, rather than by states or cities. In addition, regional organizations can promote collaborative decision-making and advance regional coordination by creating a forum for stakeholders, address problems of mutual concern, and engage in information and resource sharing.[80] Metropolitan Planning Organizations (MPO) currently perform this function for surface transportation. While MPOs do receive some federal funding for operations, they are not regional governments and generally do not execute projects. Addressing these regional problems remains difficult in the absence of more powerful regional governmental bodies. The development of more powerful regional entities could create new opportunities to address regional transportation problems.

Incorporate Performance and Accountability into Funding Decisions

Once federal goals and the federal role in surface transportation have been clarified, significant opportunities exist to incorporate performance and accountability mechanisms into federal programs. Tracking specific outcomes that are clearly linked to program goals could provide a strong foundation for holding grant recipients responsible for achieving federal objectives and measuring overall program performance. In particular, substituting specific performance measures for the federal procedural requirements that have increased over the past 50 years could help to shift federal involvement in transportation from the current process-oriented approach to a more outcome-oriented approach. Furthermore, shifting from process-oriented structures such as mode-based grant programs to performance-based programs could improve project selection by removing barriers to funding intermodal projects and giving grantees greater flexibility to select projects based on the project's ability to achieve results. Directly linking outcome-based goals to programs based on clearly defined federal interests would also help to clarify federal surface transportation policy and create a foundation for a transparent and results-based relationship between the federal government and other transportation stakeholders.

Accountability mechanisms can be incorporated into grant structures in a variety of ways. For example, grant guidelines can establish uniform outcome measures for evaluating grantees' progress toward specific goals, and grant disbursements can depend in part on the grantees' performance instead of set formulas. Thus, if reducing congestion was an established federal goal, outcome measures for congestion such as travel time reliability could be incorporated into infrastructure grants to hold states and localities responsible for meeting specific performance targets. Similarly, if increasing freight movement was an established federal goal, performance targets for freight throughput and travel time in key corridors could be built into grant programs. Performance targets could either be determined at the national level or, where appropriate, in partnership with grantees—much as DOT has established state performance goals for highway safety and motor carrier safety assistance.

Incentive grants or penalty provisions in transportation grants can also create clear links between performance and funding and help hold grantees accountable for achieving desired results. For example, the current highway and motor carrier safety incentive grants and penalty provisions can be used to increase or withhold federal grant funds based on the policy measures that states enact and the safety outcomes they achieve. Depending on the federal interest and established goals, these types of provisions could also be used in federal infrastructure grants.

In addition, a competitive selection process can help hold recipients accountable for results. For example, DOT's competitive selection process for New Starts and Small Starts transit programs require projects to meet a set of established criteria and mandates post-construction evaluations to assess project results. To better ensure that other discretionary grant programs are aligned with federal interests and achieve clearly defined federal transportation goals, Congress could establish specific project selection criteria for those programs and require that they use a competitive project selection process. For instance, key freight projects of national importance could be selected through such a competitive process that would identify those investments that are most crucial to national freight flows. DOT also recently selected metropolitan areas for Urban Partnership Agreements, which are not tied to a single grant program but do provide recipients with financial resources, regulatory flexibility, and dedicated technical support in exchange for their adoption of aggressive congestion-reduction strategies. When a national competition is not feasible, Congress could require a competitive selection process at the state or local level, such as those required for the Job Access and Reverse Commute Program. This program, however, lacks the statutorily defined selection criteria used to select projects for the New Starts and Small Starts programs.

Employ Best Tools and Approaches to Help Improve Return on Investment

The effectiveness of any overall federal program design can be increased by promoting and facilitating the use of the best tools and approaches. Within broader federal program structures that fit the principles we discuss in this report, a number of specific tools and approaches can be used to improve results and return on investment, which is increasingly necessary to meet transportation challenges as federal resources become even more constrained. We and others have identified a range of leading practices, discussed below, however their suitability varies depending on the level of federal involvement or control that policymakers desire for a given area of policy.

Rigorous economic analysis is recognized by experts as a useful tool for evaluating and comparing potential transportation projects. Benefit-cost analysis gives transportation decision makers a way to identify projects with the greatest net benefits and compare alternatives for individual projects. By translating benefits and costs into quantitative comparisons to the maximum extent feasible, these analyses provide a concrete way to link transportation investments to program goals. However, in order for benefit-cost analysis to be effective, it must be a key factor in project selection decisions and not seen simply as a requirement to be fulfilled. A complementary type of tool is outcome evaluation, which is already required for New Starts transit projects. Such evaluations would be useful in identifying leading practices and understanding project performance, especially since the available information indicates that the costs of highway and transit projects are often higher than originally anticipated.

It should be recognized, however, that benefit-cost comparisons and other analyses do not necessarily identify the federal interest—many local benefits from transportation investments are not net benefits in national terms. For example, economic development may provide financial benefits locally, but nationally the result may be largely a redistribution of resources rather than a net increase. Accordingly, in emphasizing return on federal investment, the relationship of investments to national goals must be considered along with locally-based calculations of benefit and cost.

Because current programs are generally based on specific modes, it is difficult to plan and fund intermodal links and projects that involve more than one mode, despite a consensus among experts and DOT itself that an intermodal approach is needed. A number of strategies could be used to move toward an intermodal approach. For example, policy could be changed to allow a single stream of funding to pay for all aspects of a corridor-based project—even if the improvements include such diverse measures as highway expansion, transit expansion, and congestion management. DOT recently created competitive Urban Partnership Agreements, which award grants for initiatives that address congestion through congestion pricing, transit, telecommuting, and ITS elements. Finally, decision makers cannot make full use of cross-modal project comparisons, such as those developed through benefit-cost analysis, if funding streams remain stovepiped.

Better management of existing capacity is another strategy that has proved successful, primarily on highways; it is useful because of the growing cost and, in some cases the impracticality, of building additional capacity. We have reported that implementing ITS technology can improve system performance. Congestion pricing of highways, where toll rates change according to demand, is another such leading practice. From an economic perspective, congested highways are generally "underpriced." Although the social cost of using a roadway is much higher at peak usage times, this higher cost is usually not reflected in what drivers pay. When toll rates increase with demand, some drivers respond to higher peak-period prices by changing the mode or time of their travel for trips that are flexible. This tool can increase the speed of traffic and has the potential to increase capacity as well—an evaluation of the variably priced lanes of State Route 91 in Orange County, California, showed that although the priced lanes represent only 33 percent of the capacity of State Route 91, they carry an average of 40 percent of the traffic during peak travel times. Although the Value Pricing Pilot Program encourages the use of this tool, tolling is prohibited on most Interstate highways by statute. Broader support in policy could increase the adoption of congestion pricing, improving the efficiency and performance of the system.

Public-private partnerships are another tool that may benefit public sponsors by bringing private-sector financing and efficiencies to transportation investments, among other potential advantages. Specifically, private investors can help public agencies improve the performance of existing facilities, and in some cases build new facilities without directly investing public funds. At the same time, such partnerships also present potential costs and trade-offs, but the public sector can take steps to protect the public interest. For example, when evaluating the public interest of public-private partnerships, the public sector can employ qualitative public interest tests and criteria, as well as quantitative tests such as Value for Money and Public Sector Comparators, which are used to evaluate if entering into a project as a public-private partnership is the best procurement option available.[81] Such formal assessments of public interest are used routinely in other countries, such as Australia and the United Kingdom, but use of systematic, formal processes and approaches to the identification and assessment of public interest issues has been more limited in the United States. Since public interest criteria and assessment tools generally mandate that certain aspects of the public interest are considered in public-private partnerships, if these criteria and tools are not used, then aspects of public interest might be overlooked. Although these techniques have limitations, they are able to inform public decision making—for instance, the Harris County, Texas, toll authority conducted an analysis similar to a public-sector comparator, and the results helped inform the authority's decision not to pursue a public-private approach.

Tools can also be used in designing grants to help increase the impact of federal funds. One such tool is maintenance of effort requirements, under which state or local grantees must maintain their own level of funding in order to receive federal funds. Maintenance of effort requirements could discourage states from substituting federal support for funds they themselves would otherwise have spent. However, our past work has shown that maintenance of effort requirements should be indexed to inflation and program growth in order to be effective. Matching requirements are another grant design tool that can be adjusted to increase the impact of federal programs. The allowable federal share covers a substantial portion of project costs—often 80 percent—in many transportation programs, especially for highways. Increasing the state share can help induce recipients to commit additional resources. For example, NHTSA's Occupant Protection grant program provides 75 percent federal funding the first year, but reduces the federal share to 25 percent in the fifth and sixth years to shift the primary financing responsibility to the states.

Data collection is a key tool to give policymakers information on how the transportation system is functioning. Data on the system and its individual facilities and modes are useful in their own right for decision making, but are also essential to enable other effective approaches, such as linking grant disbursements to grantees' performance. As discussed previously, DOT does not have complete data in some crucial areas; the effective use of data in safety programs, despite problems, demonstrates the potential of more comprehensive data gathering to improve evaluations and induce improved performance in the surface transportation system.

A restructured federal program could increase the application of these and other leading tools and approaches by providing incentives for or requiring their use in certain circumstances. For example, in competitive discretionary grant programs, the application of specific tools and approaches could be considered in evaluating proposals, just as the use of incentives or penalties could be considered in noncompetitive grant programs. The Motor Carrier Safety Assistance Program already employs this approach—one factor considered in awarding incentive funds is whether states provide commercial motor vehicle safety data for the national database. The use of certain tools and approaches could also simply be required in order to receive federal funds under relevant transportation grant programs. However, if federal programs were restructured to be based on performance and outcomes, states would have more incentive to implement such tools and approaches on their own. Under such a scenario, an appropriate federal role could be to facilitate their identification and dissemination.

Ensure Fiscal Sustainability

Transportation financing, and the Highway Trust Fund in particular, faces an imbalance of revenues and expenditures and other threats to its long-term sustainability. In considering sustainable sources of funds for transportation infrastructure, the user-pay principle is often cited as an appropriate pricing mechanism for transportation infrastructure.[82] While fuel taxes do reflect usage, they are not an exact user-pay mechanism and they do not convey to drivers the full costs of their use of the road. These taxes are not tied to the time when drivers actually use the road or which road they use. Taxes and fees should also be equitably assigned and reflect the different costs imposed by different users. The trucking industry pays taxes and fees for the highway infrastructure it uses, but its payments generally do not cover the costs it imposes on highways,[83] thereby giving the industry a competitive price advantage over railroads, which use infrastructure that they own and operate.[84] An alternative to fuel taxes would be to introduce mileage charges on vehicles—Oregon is pilot testing the technology to implement this approach. Finally, the use of congestion pricing to reflect the much greater cost of traveling congested highways at peak times will help optimize investment by providing market cues to policymakers.

Concerns about funding adequacy have led state and local governments to search for alternative revenue approaches, including alternative financing vehicles at the federal level, such as grant anticipation revenue vehicles, grant anticipation notes, state infrastructure banks and federal loans. These vehicles can accelerate the construction of projects, leverage federal assistance, and provide greater flexibility and more funding techniques. However, they are also different forms of debt financing. This debt ultimately must be repaid with interest, either by highway users—through tolls, fuel taxes, licensing or vehicle fees—or by the general population through increases in general fund taxes or reductions in other government services. Highway public-private partnerships show promise as an alternative, where appropriate, to help meet growing and costly transportation demands. Highway public-private partnerships have resulted in advantages, from the perspective of state and local governments, such as the construction of new infrastructure without using public funding, and obtaining funds by extracting value from existing facilities for reinvestment in public transportation and other public programs. However, there is no "free" money in public-private partnerships. Highway financing through public-private partnerships also is largely a new source of borrowed funds that must be repaid to private investors by road users, over what could be a period of several generations.[85]

Finally, the sustainability of transportation financing should also be seen in the context of broader fiscal challenges. In a time of growing structural deficits, constrained state and local budgets, and looming Social Security and Medicare spending commitments, the resources available for discretionary programs will be more limited.[86] The federal role in transportation funding must be reexamined to ensure that it is sustainable in this new fiscal reality. The long-term pressures on the Highway Trust Fund and the governmentwide problem of fiscal imbalance highlight the need for a more efficient, redesigned program based on the principles we have identified. The sustainability of surface transportation programs depends not only on the level of federal funding, but also on the allocation of funds to projects that provide the best return on investment and address national transportation priorities. Using the tools and approaches for improving transportation programs that we have discussed could also help surface transportation programs become more fiscally sustainable and more directly address national transportation priorities.

Restructuring Principles Can Help Frame the Discussion of the National Commission Report and Dissent

The National Surface Transportation Policy and Revenue Study Commission (National Commission) issued its final report in January 2008.[87] The report recommended significantly increasing the level of investment by all levels of government in surface transportation, consolidating and reorganizing the current programs, speeding project delivery, and making the current program more performance-based and mode-neutral, among other things. However, several commissioners offered a dissenting view on some of the Commission's recommendations, notably the level of investment, size of the federal role, and the revenue sources recommended. The divergent views of the commission members indicate that while there is a degree of consensus on the need to reexamine federal surface transportation programs, there is not yet a consensus on the form a restructured surface transportation program should take. The principles that we discussed for examining restructuring options are a sound basis on which this discussion can take place. These principles do not prescribe a specific approach to restructuring, but they do provide key attributes that will help ensure that a restructured surface transportation program addresses current challenges.

CONCLUSIONS

The current federal approach to addressing the nation's surface transportation problems is not working well. Despite large increases in expenditures in real terms for transportation the investment has not resulted in a commensurate improvement in the performance of nation's surface transportation system, as congestion continues to grow, and looming problems from the anticipated growth in travel demand are not being adequately addressed. The current collection of flexible but disparate programs grants that characterizes the existing approach is the result of a patchwork evolution of programs over time, not a result of a specific rationale or plan. This argues for a fundamental reexamination of the federal approach to surface transportation problems. In cases where there is a significant national interest, maintaining strong federal financial support and a more direct federal involvement in the program may be needed. In other cases, functions may best be carried by other levels of government or not at all. There may also be instances where federal financial support is desirable but a more results-oriented approach is appropriate. In addition, it is important to recognize that depending on the transportation issue and the desired goals, different options and approaches may best fit different problems. Reforming the current approach to transportation problems will take time, but a vision and strategy is needed to begin the process of transforming to a set of policies and programs to effectively address the nation's transportation needs and priorities. The current system evolved over many years and involves different modes, infrastructure and safety issues, and extends widely into the operations of state and local governments.

Given the proliferation of programs and goals previously discussed, refocusing federal programs is needed to address the shortfalls of the current approach. Focusing federal programs around a clear federal interest is key. Well-defined goals based on identified areas of federal interest would establish what federal participation in surface transportation is designed to accomplish. A clearly defined federal role in achieving these goals would give policymakers the ability to direct federal resources proportionately to the level of national interest. Once this is accomplished, a basis exists to reexamine the current patchwork of programs, test their continued relevance and relative priority, potentially devolve programs and policies that are outdated or ineffective, and modernize those programs and policies that remain relevant.

Once those areas of federal interest are known, tying federal funds to performance and having mechanisms to test whether goals are met would help create incentives to state and local governments to improve their performance and the performance of the transportation system. Both incentive programs and sanctions are possible models for better tying performance to outcomes. Having more federal programs operate on a competitive basis and projects selected based on potential benefits could also help tie federal funds to performance.

There also is a need to improve the use of analytical tools in the selection and evaluation of the performance of projects. Better use of tools such as benefit-cost analysis and using return on investment as a criterion for the selection of individual projects can help identify the best projects. Specifically, the use of a return on investment framework will help to emphasize that federal financial commitments to transportation infrastructure projects are, in fact, long-term capital investments designed to achieve tangible results in a transparent fashion.

Finally, a fundamental problem exists in the fiscal sustainability of surface transportation programs as a result of the impending shortfall in the Highway Trust Fund. The trust fund is the primary source of federal support to state and local governments across highways, transit, and surface transportation safety programs. This fiscal crisis is fundamentally based on the balance of revenues and expenditures in the fund, and thus either reduced expenditures, increased revenues, or a combination of the two is now needed to bring the fund back into balance. Finally, given the scope of needed transformation, the shifts in policies and programs may need to be done incrementally or on a pilot basis to gain practical lessons for a coherent, sustainable, and effective national program and financing structure to best serve the nation for the 21st century.

Matter for Congressional Consideration

To improve the effectiveness of the federal investment in surface transportation, meet the nation's transportation needs, and ensure a sustainable commitment to transportation infrastructure, Congress should consider reexamining and refocusing surface transportation programs to be responsive to these principles so that they:

- have well-defined goals with direct links to an identified federal interest and role,
- institute processes to make grantees more accountable by establishing more performance-based links between funding and program outcomes,
- institute tools and approaches to that emphasize the return on the federal investment, and
- address the current imbalance between federal surface transportation revenues and spending.

JayEtta Z. Hecker,
Director, Physical Infrastructure Issues

Appendix I: Objectives, Scope, and Methodology

We were asked to (1) provide an historical overview of the federal role in surface transportation and the goals and structures of federal surface transportation programs funded by the Highway Trust Fund, (2) summarize conclusions from our prior work on the structure and performance of these and other federal programs, and (3) identify principles to help assess options for focusing the future federal role and the structure of federal surface transportation programs.

We focused our work on programs funded by the Highway Trust Fund (HTF) because it is the primary vehicle for federal financing of surface transportation, receiving nearly all federal fuel tax revenue; it is also a focus of most proposals to reform the current federal role. We examined the Federal Highway Administration (FHWA), Federal Motor Carrier Safety Administration (FMCSA), Federal Transit Administration (FTA) and National Highway Traffic Safety Administration (NHTSA) as part of this study; we did not look at two other DOT agencies that receive HTF funds, the Research and Innovative Technology Administration (RITA) and the Federal Railroad Administration (FRA). RITA was excluded because it focuses on federal research, in contrast to our focus on federal-state programs; FRA was excluded because the portion of HTF funds that it receives is so small that it cannot be compared to the other operating agencies.

To provide an historical overview of the federal role in surface transportation and the goals and structures of federal surface transportation programs, we drew information from statutes, especially transportation authorization laws; regulations; budget documents; agency reports; and literature on transportation policy by outside experts. We interviewed officials in DOT's modal administrations, including FHWA, FMCSA, FTA, and NHTSA in order to help clarify agency goals, roles and structures. We also interviewed representatives of stakeholder groups such as the American Association of State Highway and Transportation Officials (AASHTO) and the American Public Transit Association (APTA).

To describe conclusions that we and others have drawn about the current structure and performance of these federal programs, we reviewed relevant GAO reports on specific transportation programs, as well as reports that looked at broader issues of performance measurement, oversight, grant design, and other related issues. We also reviewed reports, policy statements, and other materials from stakeholder groups and other organizations. Additionally, we reviewed materials from hearings held by the National Surface

Transportation Policy and Revenue Study Commission. Finally, we sought the views of transportation experts, including the 22 who participated in a forum convened by the Comptroller General in May 2007, that included public officials, private-sector executives, researchers, and others.

To review policy options for addressing the federal role, we identified options from previous proposals, both those originating in Congress and presidential administrations, as well as those presented by stakeholder groups such as AASHTO. We also reviewed options discussed in previous GAO reports, as well as testimony and other materials generated by the National Surface Transportation Policy and Revenue Study Commission, which the Congress also tasked to examine the federal approach to surface transportation programs.

In addition, to complement our appendix III discussion of the implications of turning over responsibility for surface transportation to the states, we analyzed the potential fiscal impact of turning over most elements of the federal transportation program to the states. We obtained DOT data on state grant disbursements and calculated total federal grant receipts for each state and the District of Columbia. We limited our analysis to grant programs funded by the HTF, because the federal fuel taxes that would be eliminated or sharply reduced under this scenario are deposited almost exclusively in the HTF. We also omitted discretionary grants because they are a small portion of federal transportation grants and often vary significantly from year to year in a given state. Separately, we obtained state fuel consumption data from DOT. In order to calculate the extent to which individual states would have to raise their fuel taxes to maintain the same level of spending if federal grants were eliminated, we divided the total grant receipts (as described above) for each state by the number of gallons of highway fuel used in that state in the prior year. This calculation yielded the per-gallon increase in state taxes that would be needed to maintain spending, assuming it would be implemented evenly across all types of fuel. Because diesel and gasoline are taxed at different federal rates, and represent different shares of total usage in each state, we used a weighted average to calculate the current effective per-gallon federal fuel tax rate in each state. We then expressed the per-gallon tax rate results in terms of change from the current federal tax rate. Where we had not previously assessed the reliability of the source data, we conducted a limited data reliability analysis and found the data suitable for the purpose of this analysis.

We conducted this performance audit between April 2007 and February 2008 in accordance with Generally Accepted Government Auditing Standards. Those standards require that we plan and perform the audit to obtain sufficient, appropriate evidence that provides a reasonable basis for our findings and conclusions based on our audit objectives. We believe that the evidence obtained provides a reasonable basis for our findings and conclusions based on our audit objectives.

APPENDIX II: OVERVIEW OF FEDERAL SURFACE TRANSPORTATION PROGRAMS

Federal Highway Infrastructure Assistance Since 1956

Current Programs

Federal assistance for highway infrastructure is distributed through several grant programs, known collectively as the Federal-Aid Highway Program. Both Congress and DOT have established multiple broad policy goals for the Federal-Aid Highway Program, which provides financial and technical assistance to states to construct, preserve, and improve eligible federal-aid highways. The program's current goals include safety, efficiency, mobility, congestion relief, interstate and international commerce, national security, economic growth, environmental stewardship, and sustaining the nation's quality of life.

The Federal-Aid Highway Program currently consists of seven core formula grant programs and several smaller formula and discretionary grant programs. The majority of Highway Trust Fund revenues are distributed through the core formula grant programs to the states for a variety of purposes, including road construction and improvements, Interstate highway and bridge repair, air pollution mitigation, highway safety, and equity considerations. Broad flexibility provisions allow states to transfer funds between core highway programs and to the Federal Transit Administration (FTA) for eligible transit projects. Highway Trust Fund revenues are also distributed through the smaller formula and discretionary grant programs, which cover a wide range of projects, including border infrastructure, recreational trails, and safe routes to schools. Congress has also designated funds for specific projects. For example, according to the Transportation Research Board, SAFETEA-LU—the most recent reauthorization legislation—contained over 5,000 dedicated spending provisions.

The Federal-Aid Highway Program is administered through a federal-state partnership. The federal government, through FHWA, provides financial assistance, policy direction, technical expertise, and some oversight.[88] FHWA headquarters provides leadership, oversight, and policy direction for the agency, FHWA state division offices deliver the bulk of the program's technical expertise and oversight functions, and five FHWA regional service resource centers provide guidance, training, and additional technical expertise to the division offices. In turn, state and local governments execute the programs by matching and distributing federal funds; planning, selecting, and supervising projects; and complying with federal requirements. Currently, based on stewardship agreements with each state, FHWA exercises full oversight on a limited number of federal-aid projects. States are required to oversee all federal-aid highway projects that are not on the National Highway System, and states oversee design and construction phases of other projects based on an agreement between FHWA and the state. FHWA also reviews state management and planning processes. Many state and local government processes are driven by federal requirements, including not only highway-specific requirements for transportation planning and maintenance, but also environmental review requirements and labor standards that are the result of separate federal legislation designed to address social and environmental goals.

Changes over Time

Since its reauthorization under the Federal-Aid Highway Act of 1956, the Federal-Aid Highway Program has grown in size, scope, and complexity as federal goals for the program have expanded. In 1956, the primary focus of the Federal-Aid Highway Program was to help states finance and construct the Interstate Highway System to meet the nation's needs for efficient travel, economic development, and national defense. The Federal-aid Highway Program made funds available to states for road construction and improvements through four formula programs—one program for each of four eligible road categories—with a particular focus on the Interstate system. Yet the Federal-Aid Highway Program has also served as a mechanism to achieve other societal goals. For example, the 1956 Act requires that states adhere to federal wage and labor standards for any state construction project using federal-aid funds. In successive reauthorizations of the program, Congress has increased program requirements to achieve other societal goals such as civil rights, environmental protection, urban planning, and economic development.

Besides increasing compliance requirements, Congress has authorized new grant programs to achieve expanded program objectives. For example, Congress authorized new core grant programs to address Interstate highway maintenance, environmental goals, and safety. In response to controversy over the distribution of highway funds between states that pay more in federal taxes and fees than they receive in federal-aid (donor states) and states that receive more in federal-aid than they contribute (donee states), Congress established and strengthened equity programs that guarantee states a minimum relative return on their payments into the Highway Account of HTF. Additionally, Congress has further expanded the program's scope by authorizing highway funds for additional purposes and uses, such as highway beautification, historic preservation, and bicycle trails.

The federal-state partnership has evolved as programs have changed to give states and localities greater funding flexibility. For example, in 1991, when Interstate construction was nearly complete, Congress restructured the Federal-aid Highway Program to promote a more efficient and flexible distribution of funds. Specifically, under the Intermodal Surface Transportation Efficiency Act of 1991 (ISTEA),[89] Congress substantially increased flexibility by consolidating road-category grant programs, creating a surface transportation block grant, and establishing broad flexible fund transfer provisions between highway programs and transit—a structure that remains today. At the same time, Congress altered the established federal-state partnership by increasing the authority of metropolitan planning organizations—local governmental planning bodies—in federally mandated planning processes.

The federal-state partnership has further evolved as Congress has delegated federal oversight responsibilities to state and local governments, but has assumed a greater role in project selection. When Interstate construction began, the federal government provided direct oversight during the construction and maintenance phases of projects and ensured that the states complied with federal requirements. By 1973, states could self-certify compliance with most federal grant requirements, and during the 1990s, Congress further expanded this authority to allow states and FHWA to cooperatively determine the appropriate level of oversight for federally funded projects, including some Interstate projects. While reducing the federal role in oversight, Congress has increased its role in project selection—traditionally a state and local responsibility—through congressional directives. For example, according to the Transportation Research Board, there were over 5,000 directives in the latest reauthorization from 2005, up from 1,850 in 1998 and 11 in 1982.

As the Federal-Aid Highway Program has grown in size and complexity, so too has the federal administrative structure although some shifting or consolidation of responsibilities has occurred. Before FHWA was created in 1967, its predecessor, the Bureau of Public Roads, established a decentralized administrative structure and a field office in each state, reflecting the close partnership between the federal government and the states. Moreover, as the number of the Federal-Aid Highway Program requirements and the scope of the program increased, the agency, which initially had an engineering focus, hired a wide range of specialists including: economists, landscape architects, planners, historians, ecologists, safety experts, civil rights experts, and others. When DOT was formed in 1967, new motor carrier and traffic and vehicle safety functions were assigned to FHWA. These functions have since shifted to NHTSA and FMCSA, although FHWA continues to collaborate on these issues and retains responsibility for highway infrastructure-related safety projects and programs. In 1998, FHWA consolidated its organization by eliminating its nine regional offices and establishing regional service resource centers, as well as devolving responsibility for state projects and programs entirely to the FHWA division offices in each state. For fiscal year 2009, FHWA requested funding for 2,861 full-time equivalent staff divided between headquarters, 5 regional service resource centers and 55 division offices.[90]

Federal Transit Assistance

Current Programs

Both Congress and DOT have established multiple broad policy goals for FTA, which provides financial and technical assistance to local and state public agencies to build, maintain, and operate mass transportation systems. FTA's current statutory goals include (1) promoting the development of efficient and coordinated urban transportation systems that maximize mobility, support economic development, and reduce environmental and energy consumption impacts, and (2) providing mobility for vulnerable populations in both urban and rural areas. DOT's six strategic goals also apply to FTA: safety, congestion mitigation, global connectivity, environmental stewardship, security and preparedness, and organizational excellence.

Currently, FTA divides its major capital and operating assistance programs into two categories: formula and bus grants, which are funded entirely from HTF's Mass Transit Account,[91] and capital investment grants, which are financed using general revenue. The formula and bus grants provide capital and operating assistance[92] to transit agencies and states through a combination of seven relatively large and five smaller formula and discretionary grants. Under these grants, the federal government generally provides 80 percent of the funding and the locality provides 20 percent, with certain exceptions.[93] The capital investment grants provide discretionary capital assistance for the construction of new fixed-guideway and corridor systems and extensions of existing systems. Funds for new fixed-guideway systems are distributed through the New Starts and Small Starts grant programs and are awarded to individual projects through a competitive selection process.[94] Although the statutory federal match for the New Starts and Small Starts programs is 80 percent, agency officials stated the actual federal match is closer to 50 percent due to high levels of state and local investment and the competitive selection process that favors projects that require a lower federal match. FTA also provides financial support for research and planning activities. Funds for research are allocated on a discretionary basis out of the General Fund, and planning funds are taken from the Mass Transit Account of the Highway Trust Fund and distributed to states by formula. In addition to the funding they obtain through these programs, states may transfer a portion of certain highway program funds to FTA for eligible transit expenses. According to the most recent DOT data, in 2004, 28.1 percent of the funding for transit was system-generated through fares or other charges, and the remaining funds came from local (34.6 percent), state (19.7 percent), and federal (17.6 percent) sources. Approximately 75 percent of federal transit assistance is directed to capital investments, and the remainder is directed to other eligible expenses such as operating expenses.

In contrast to federal highway infrastructure programs, which are administered through a federal-state partnership, federal transit programs are generally administered through a federal-local partnership, although rural programs are administered at the state level. The federal government, through FTA headquarters and 10 FTA regional offices, provides financial assistance, establishes requirements, performs oversight, and conducts research. Grant recipients such as local transit agencies are responsible for matching federal funds and for planning, selecting, and executing projects while complying with federal requirements. The degree of federal oversight varies across programs and among grant recipients. Currently, full federal oversight[95] is limited to major capital projects that cost over $100 million, and local and state grant recipients are allowed to self-certify their compliance with certain federal laws and regulations. For example, FTA conducts periodic reviews of program management processes for recipients of Block Grants Program (Urbanized Area Formula Grants) funds and provides direct project management oversight for recipients of New Starts funding.[96] In addition, FTA conducts discretionary reviews of grantees' compliance with requirements in other areas such as financial management or civil rights and uses a rating system to determine the level of oversight needed for each grantee.[97] FTA employees work with external contractors to conduct project management and program management process reviews. For fiscal year 2009, FTA requested funding for 526 full-time-equivalent staff, divided among its 10 regional offices and headquarters.

Changes over Time

From the modern transit program's inception as part of the Urban Mass Transportation Act of 1964 (UMTA), Congress justified federal funding for mass transportation capital improvements as a means to address pressing urban problems such as urban decay, traffic congestion, and poor development planning. Federal capital assistance was distributed to local governments on a discretionary basis to help urban areas improve and expand urban mass transportation systems. Congress also established federal transit programs to achieve other societal goals. For example, UMTA required grant recipients to provide labor protections for transit employees and relocation assistance for individuals displaced by transit projects.[98] Later federal legislation increased grant requirements to achieve other societal goals such as civil rights, environmental protection, and economic development.

In addition to increasing compliance requirements, Congress has authorized new grant programs and broadened program eligibility requirements to promote expanding objectives. For example, federal transit assistance expanded during the 1970s to include grant programs designed to meet social and transportation-related goals such as: improving mobility in rural areas[99] and making public transportation more accessible for the elderly and the disabled.[100] More recently, Congress has further broadened the scope of programs to include making transportation to jobs more accessible for welfare recipients and low-income individuals[101] and providing transit service within public parks and lands.[102] Although federal transit funding was initially provided on a discretionary basis from the General Fund of the Treasury, many of the newer programs make funds available through formulas, and highway user fees have replaced general revenues as the major source of transit assistance since the creation of the Mass Transit Account of the Highway Trust Fund in 1983. In addition, Congress has broadened the scope of federal transit assistance to include operating expenses and capital maintenance as well as capital expenses. For example, concerns about growing operating deficits among transit agencies led Congress to authorize the use of federal funds for transit operating expenses in 1974. Although federal support for operating expenses in urbanized areas has since declined, operating assistance is still available for areas with a population of less than 200,000.

The federal-local relationship in transit has evolved as Congress has expanded federal involvement in transit and increased state and local government authority and flexibility in using federal funds. For example, in 1978, Congress expanded federal transit assistance to rural areas and made state governments responsible for receiving and distributing these funds. According to agency officials, states previously played a limited role in transit projects because the federal government worked directly with urban areas and transit agencies. In 1991, Congress increased local authority by expanding the role of metropolitan planning organizations in project selection and transportation planning. At the same time, Congress substantially increased state and local authority to transfer funds between highway and transit programs. The combination of additional transfer authority and the gradual shift toward apportioning funds through formulas rather than individual project awards has increased flexibility for both state and local transit grant recipients. In addition, state and local government oversight responsibilities have increased for federal transit grants, much as they have for federal highway infrastructure grants, with self-certification procedures for compliance with federal laws and regulations, and additional federal compliance requirements such as those for environmental review.

Federal Highway Safety and Motor Carrier Safety Assistance

Current Programs

Federal highway safety and motor carrier safety assistance programs are separately administered by NHTSA and FMCSA. The primary statutory policy goals of these programs are directed to reducing accidents, and the bulk of NHTSA's and FMCSA's financial support and research, education, rulemaking, and enforcement activities fall under DOT's strategic goal of improving safety. Although FHWA and FTA exercise rulemaking authority in the administration of their programs, rulemaking and enforcement are primary tools that NHTSA and FMCSA use to reduce accidents and their associated damages.

Highway safety and motor carrier safety grant programs are similarly organized. Both use a basic formula grant to provide funding to states for safety programs, enforcement activities, and related expenditures, coupled with several targeted discretionary grants. Currently, almost 40 percent of authorized federal highway safety assistance is distributed by formula to states through the State and Community Highway Safety Grant Program (Section 402), which supports a wide range of highway safety initiatives at the state and local level. This basic program is augmented by several smaller discretionary grant programs that mostly target funds to improve safety through the use of measures such as seat belts and child safety restraints, among others.[103] Most of these discretionary grants provide states with financial incentives for meeting specific performance or safety activity criteria. For example, to be eligible for Alcohol-Impaired Driving Countermeasures Incentive grants, most states must either have a low alcohol fatality rate or meet programmatic criteria for enforcement, outreach, and other related activities.[104] In addition to discretionary grants, Congress has authorized highway safety provisions that penalize states by either transferring or withholding state highway infrastructure funds from states that do not comply with certain federal provisions. These penalty provisions can provide a substantial amount of additional funding for state safety activities. For example, in 2007, penalty provisions transferred over $217 million of federal highway infrastructure assistance to highway safety programs in the 19 states and Puerto Rico that were penalized for failure to meet federal criteria for either open container requirements or minimum penalties for repeat offenders for driving while intoxicated or under the influence.[105]

The majority of federal motor carrier safety funds are distributed by formula to states through the Motor Carrier Safety Assistance Program (MSCAP), which provides financial assistance to states for the enforcement of federal motor carrier safety and hazardous materials regulations. In addition, several smaller discretionary programs are targeted to achieve specific goals such as data system improvements and border enforcement, among others. Some of these grants require states to maintain a level of funding for eligible motor carrier safety activities to reduce the potential for federal funds to replace state financial support.[106] Finally, FMCSA sets aside MCSAP funds to support high-priority areas such as audits of new motor carrier operations. Unlike the highway safety grants, most of these discretionary programs do not have statutorily defined performance or outcome-related eligibility criteria, and funds are allocated at the agency's discretion.[107] States that do not comply with federal commercial driver licensing requirements may have up to 5 percent of their annual highway construction funds withheld in the first fiscal year and 10 percent in the second fiscal year of violation. However, these withheld funds, unlike the funds withheld or transferred under some highway safety penalty provisions, are not available to the penalized states for motor carrier safety activities.

Like highway infrastructure grants, most federal highway safety and motor carrier safety grants are jointly administered through a federal-state partnership. Through NHTSA and FMCSA, the federal government provides funds, establishes and enforces regulations, collects and analyzes data, performs oversight, conducts research, performs educational outreach, and provides technical assistance. In turn, states provide matching funds, develop and execute safety and enforcement plans and programs, distribute funds to other governmental partners, collect and analyze data, and comply with federal grant and reporting requirements. Both NHTSA and FMCSA use a performance-based approach to grant oversight. Each agency reviews state safety plans, which establish specific performance goals, and then monitors states' progress towards achieving their goals. Because these efforts rely on the accuracy and completeness of state safety data, both NHTSA and FMCSA emphasize state data collection and analysis in the administration of their grant programs. In addition to their annual safety performance reviews, NHTSA and FMCSA conduct periodic management and compliance reviews of grant recipients.

NHTSA and FMCSA also each have a substantial regulatory role. NHTSA establishes and enforces safety standards for passenger vehicles in areas such as tire safety, occupant protection devices, and crashworthiness, as well as issuing fuel economy standards. FMCSA establishes and enforces standards for motor carrier vehicles and operations, hazardous materials, household goods movement, commercial vehicle operator medical requirements, and international motor carrier safety. NHTSA conducts testing, inspection, analysis, and investigations to identify noncompliance with vehicle safety standards, and if necessary, initiates a product recall. FMCSA conducts compliance reviews of motor carriers' operations at their places of business as well as roadside inspections of drivers and vehicles, and can assess a variety of penalties including fines and cessation orders for noncompliance. Both NHTSA and FMCSA rely on data to target their enforcement activities.

NHTSA and FMCSA use different organizational structures to administer their grant programs. NHTSA has both a headquarters office and 10 regional offices. Headquarters staff develop policy and programs and provide technical assistance to regional staff. Regional staff review and approve state safety plans, and provide technical assistance. According to agency officials, since NHTSA does not provide the same level of technical assistance as FHWA, a regional rather than a state division structure is appropriate to NHTSA's needs. For fiscal year 2009, NHTSA requested funding for 635 full-time-equivalent staff divided among its headquarters and regional offices. Similar to FHWA, FMCSA has a field structure of 4 regional service centers and 52 division offices. Headquarters staff establish and communicate agency priorities, issue policy guidance, and carry out financial management activities. Regional service centers act as an intermediary between headquarters and division offices by clarifying policy and organizing training and goal-setting meetings for MSCAP grants. Division offices have primary responsibility for overseeing state motor carrier safety programs and work closely with the states to develop commercial vehicle safety plans. These offices also monitor state progress and grant expenditures. For fiscal year 2009, FMCSA requested funding for 1119 full-time equivalent staff divided among its headquarters and field offices.

Changes over Time

In broad terms, both federal highway safety and motor carrier safety programs have followed a similar path since their inception. Both federal highway safety and motor carrier safety activities were components of the federal highway program before separate modal agencies were established within DOT. Both state-assistance programs began as a single basic formula grant that was then expanded to include smaller targeted discretionary grants. Additionally, Congress has given states greater flexibility to set their own priorities within the parameters of national safety goals, and both NHTSA and FMCSA have adopted a performance-based approach to grant oversight. Although broader environmental and social goals have had less of an impact on federal safety grant programs, the scope and administrative complexity of highway safety and motor carrier safety regulatory functions has expanded to incorporate these goals.

Because of growing concerns about vehicle safety and traffic accidents, the National Traffic and Motor Vehicle Safety Act and Highway Safety Act established highway safety as a separate grant program and regulatory function in 1966. Two major grants provided federal highway safety assistance in 1966: the State and Community Highway Safety (Section 402) grants and Highway Safety Research and Development (Section 403) grants. Section 402 grants distributed federal assistance to states by formula to support the creation of state highway safety programs and the implementation of countermeasures to address behavioral factors in accidents. State safety programs were required to meet several uniform federal standards to be eligible for funding and avoid withholding penalties. Section 403 grants provided discretionary federal funding for research, training, technical assistance, and demonstration projects. Although originally administered by the Department of Commerce, federal highway safety grants and regulatory authority were transferred to the Federal Highway Administration (FHWA) upon its creation in 1967. In 1970, FHWA's National Highway Safety Bureau became a separate agency within DOT and was renamed the National Highway Traffic Safety Administration.

Since 1966, Congress has increased state and local government authority and flexibility to set and fund safety priorities by removing some federal grant requirements and restrictions, and by relying more on incentive-based discretionary grants to achieve national safety goals. For example, the uniform federal standards first established in 1966 for state highway safety programs funded by Section 402 grants became guidelines in 1987, and in 1998, Congress amended federal oversight procedures from direct oversight of state safety programs to selective oversight of state safety goals based on state performance. Additionally Congress has removed dedicated spending restrictions on Section 402 funds and replaced some of them with separate incentive grant programs. For example, provisions that required a percentage of Section 402 funds to be dedicated to 55 mph speed limit enforcement, school bus safety, child safety restraints, and seat belt use have been discontinued. Some of the priorities addressed by these spending restrictions have become separate incentive programs designed to reward state performance and activities in these areas rather than limit the availability of Section 402 funds.[108] However, in certain priority areas, Congress has provided additional incentives for state compliance by authorizing penalty provisions to withhold or transfer state highway infrastructure funds for failure to meet specific safety criteria.

Unlike federal highway and transit infrastructure grants, NHTSA's grants have not been as directly affected by emerging national social and environmental goals, although Congress has incorporated these goals into NHTSA's regulatory processes. States must comply with several broad federal requirements such as nondiscrimination policies to receive federal safety funds. However, these requirements have not increased the administrative complexity of highway safety grants to the same extent as infrastructure grants because most safety activities funded through NHTSA do not require construction. For example, state safety activities such as enforcement of traffic laws and accident data collection are generally not subject to construction-related requirements such as environmental assessments and construction contract labor standards which apply to highway and transit infrastructure programs. Similarly, Congress has added only one targeted highway safety grant program to specifically address a social goal unrelated to safety—the reduction of racial profiling in law enforcement—and one grant provision requiring states to ensure accessibility for disabled persons on all new roadside curbs. In contrast, federal social and environmental goals have had a greater impact on NHTSA's regulatory processes. For example, in response to the energy crisis during the 1970s, Congress gave NHTSA authority to set corporate average fuel economy standards. Furthermore, the agency's rulemaking process is subject to executive orders and regulations designed to meet legislatively established social and environmental goals such as NEPA, the Paperwork Reduction Act, energy effects, and unfunded mandates.

Before FMCSA was established as a separate modal administration within DOT in 1999, federal motor carrier safety functions were administered by both the former Interstate Commerce Commission and FHWA. Until 1982, the federal government regulated motor carrier safety but did not provide financial assistance to states for enforcement. The Surface Transportation Act of 1982 authorized the Secretary of Transportation to make grants to the states for the development or implementation of state programs to enforce federal and state commercial motor vehicle regulations. This authorization became the foundation for the basic MCSAP grant. Since 1982, Congress has expanded the number and scope of motor carrier grant programs and requirements to meet emerging areas of concern, including border enforcement, vehicle and driver information systems, commercial driver license oversight, and safety data collection. Congress has also set-aside grant funds for purposes such as high-priority areas and new entry audits. Additionally, grant eligibility requirements have increased. For example, state enforcement plans must meet 24 criteria to be eligible for a basic MCSAP grant today, compared with 7 criteria when the program started in 1982. Although grant requirements have increased, Congress has given states some flexibility to set enforcement priorities by restructuring the programs to become performance-based and allowing states to tailor their activities to meet their particular circumstances, provided these activities work toward national goals. Additionally, FMCSA follows a performance-based approach to grant oversight.

Like highway safety grant programs, motor carrier safety grant programs have undergone fewer structural and administrative changes in response to emerging national social and environmental concerns than have federal highway and transit infrastructure grant programs. Although states must adhere to broad requirements to receive federal funds, some of these requirements, such as those calling for environmental assessments, are not relevant for safety activities that do not involve construction. Furthermore, Congress has not added any specific grant programs or grant requirements exclusive to motor carrier safety assistance that directly address other social and environmental goals.

FMCSA's regulatory and enforcement scope has expanded considerably over time. Much of this expansion is related directly to safety, but Congress has also incorporated other policy goals into FMCSA's regulatory functions. For example, hazardous materials transport, commercial driver licensing programs, and operator medical requirements have become additional areas of FMCSA regulation and enforcement that directly relate to safety. However, Congress has also given FMCSA regulatory authority for consumer protection in interstate household goods movement, which does not specifically address reducing motor carrier-related fatalities. Additionally, FMCSA's rulemaking process is subject to executive orders and regulations designed to meet legislatively established social and environmental goals.

Appendix III: Implications of "Turning Back" Surface Transportation Programs and Revenues to the States

A fundamental reexamination of surface transportation programs begins with identifying issues in which there is a strong federal interest and determining what the federal goals should be related to those issues. Once the federal interest and goals have been identified, the federal role in relation to state and local governments can be clearly defined. For issues in which there is a strong federal interest, ongoing federal financial support and direct federal involvement could help meet federal goals. But for issues in which there is little or no federal interest, programs and activities may better be devolved to other levels of government or to other parties.

In some cases, it may be appropriate to "turn back" activities and programs to state and local governments if they are best suited to perform them. Many surface transportation programs have a dedicated source of funding, that is, they are funded from a dedicated fund—the Highway Trust Fund. Devolving federal responsibility for programs could entail simultaneously relinquishing the federal revenue base, in this case, revenues that go into the Highway Trust Fund.[109] A turnback of federal programs, responsibilities, and funding would have many implications and would require careful decisions to be made at the federal, state, and local levels. These implications and decisions include the following:

- At the federal level, it would need to be determined (1) what functions would remain and (2) how federal agencies would be structured and staffed to deliver those programs. In deciding what functions would remain, the extent of federal interest in the activity compared to the extent of state or local interest should be considered. Furthermore, in deciding how to staff and deliver programs, for agencies with a large field presence, like FHWA and FMCSA, it would have to be determined what their responsibilities would be.
- At all levels of government, it would need to be determined how to handle a variety of other federal requirements that are tied to federal funds, such as the requirements for state highway safety programs related to impaired driving and state and metropolitan planning roles. At the federal level, Congress would have to decide whether to keep the requirements, and if so, how to ensure that they are met without federal funds to provide incentives or to withhold with sanctions. If the effect of a turnback is to relinquish requirements, then states and localities would have to decide what kind of planning and other requirements they want to have and how to implement them.
- At the state and local levels, it would need to be determined (1) whether to replace revenues with state taxes and (2) what type of programs to finance. Deciding whether to replace federal revenues with state taxes may be difficult because states also face fiscal challenges and replacing revenues would have different effects on different states. For example, if states decided to raise fuel taxes, some states could simply replace the current federal tax with an equivalent state tax, but other states might have to levy additional state taxes at a much higher level than the current federal tax. States would also have options of using other revenue sources such as vehicle registration fees or expanded use of tolling. With states deciding what type of programs to continue there is no way to predict which federal programs would be replaced with equivalent state programs. Finally, while states may gain flexibility in how they deliver projects, in some cases states could actually lose some

flexibility they currently have using federal funds—for example, the flexibility to move funds between highway and transit programs.

A Turnback Would Require Deciding What Federal Functions Would Remain and How Federal Agencies Would Be Structured to Deliver Those Functions

The functions that would remain at the federal level would be determined by the level of federal interest. Some functions are financed from the Highway Trust Fund but exist because of broader commitments. For example, the federal government owns land managed by agencies such as the Bureau of Land Management, Bureau of Indian Affairs, and the Forest Service. The responsibility for funding and overseeing construction of these roads is within DOT, specifically within FHWA's federal lands division. It is unlikely that the federal government would assign the responsibilities to construct roads on federal lands to state or local government. Thus, the decision may be whether, in a restructured federal program, to continue to finance this responsibility from federal gas taxes or shift responsibility to the managing agency, but not whether the responsibility would be turned over to another level of government. In another area, the federal government takes a defined role in response to disasters, as exemplified in the Robert T. Stafford Disaster Relief and Emergency Assistance Act.[110] Similarly, the Emergency Relief program provides funds to states and other federal agencies for the repair or reconstruction of federal-aid highways that have been damaged or destroyed by natural disasters or catastrophic failures. This is a long-established federal function and Congress has provided funds for the emergency repair of roads since at least 1928. Given the ongoing federal commitment to respond to disasters it is likely that emergency relief would remain a federal function. Devolving other programs would depend on how the federal interest and the federal role were defined. For example, maintaining systems such as Interstate highways or the National Highway System could be designated as part of the national interest.

The effect of various turnback scenarios on DOT modal agencies would depend on how expansively the federal role is defined. For example, FHWA in fiscal year 2008 had about 1,400 personnel in field offices, or about half of its total staff. FHWA maintains a division office in each state that provides oversight of state programs and projects as defined in a stewardship agreement between the state and the division office. The division offices may provide project-level oversight in some cases or delegate that responsibility to the state. Division offices also review state DOTs' programs and processes to ensure that states have adequate controls in place to effectively manage federally assisted projects. Thus, if a substantial portion of federal highway programs is turned back to the states, the greatest effect might be felt at the division office level, as the oversight activities of these offices might largely be considered for elimination. However, certain functions and offices could remain, such as the Office of Federal Lands Highways, which provides funding and oversight for highways on federal lands and constitutes, including both headquarters and field, about one-fourth of all FHWA staff. Other functions, such as Emergency Relief program or environmental oversight, might remain and require a field office presence of some type. A reduced or eliminated division office structure might be warranted, or residual functions might suggest a regional structure. Even under an extensive turnback scenario, FHWA might retain a technical support function, along with its five existing resource center locations. Effects on other DOT agencies of a general turnback of transportation grants would vary and would hinge on what activities the agencies would continue to perform. For example, assuming FMCSA's inspection activities continue, the significant numbers of field staff required to perform those functions would remain. If NHTSA's safety grants to the states for purposes such as reducing impaired driving or increasing seat belt use were turned back, the functions of NHTSA field staff would need to be reviewed, as these staff would no longer be needed for grant oversight. However, NHTSA could still retain its regulatory and research responsibilities, such as those related to fuel economy standards, automotive recalls, and crash testing, among others, and might need to retain those staff.

The Status of Other Federal Requirements Tied to Federal Funds Would Need to Be Decided

In some programs, federal funding is contingent on actions taken by states. In the highway safety area the federal government has applied both incentives and sanctions based on state actions. In the past these strategies have been used to encourage states to enact laws that establish a minimum drinking age of 21 years and a maximum blood alcohol level of 0.08 to determine impaired driving ability. In addition, Safety Belt Performance Grants promote national priorities by providing financial incentives for meeting certain specific performance or safety activity criteria. Penalty provisions such as those associated with Open Container laws and Motor Carrier Safety Assistance Program grants promote federal priorities by transferring or withholding the state's federal funds if states do not comply. If such programs were turned back to the states and if these incentive and sanction programs were eliminated, there would not appear to be a substitute basis for the federal government to influence state actions.

Extensive state and metropolitan planning requirements could be affected by a turnback of the highway program. Federal laws and requirements specify an overall approach for transportation planning that states and regional organizations must follow in order to receive federal funds. This approach includes involving numerous stakeholders, identifying state and regional goals, developing long- and short-range state and metropolitan planning documents, and ensuring that a wide range of transportation planning factors are considered in the process. Without this structure, it is not clear what form planning processes might take at the state level, or what role, if any, the federal government would have in relation to planning activities. At the local level, metropolitan planning organizations (MPO) came into being largely as result of federal planning requirements, and MPO activities are in part funded through the current federal-aid program. In general, the role MPOs would play after a turnback of the federal program is unclear and would need to be redefined. The status of existing planning requirements and the amount of federal funding for metropolitan planning organizations (MPOs), if any, would have to be determined. If the effect of a turnback is to relinquish requirements, then states and localities would have to decide what kind of planning and other requirements they want to have and how to establish those requirements as a matter of policy.

In addition, a turnback of federal surface transportation programs would necessitate a review of which federal requirements still apply. As a condition of receiving federal funds, states must adhere to federal regulations such as those covering contracting practices.[111] For example, under the current highway program states must comply with the provisions of the Disadvantaged Business Enterprise Program, which requires that a certain percentage of contracts be awarded to socially or economically disadvantaged firms such as minority and women-owned businesses.[112] Yet another area requiring review would be the applicability of federal environmental requirements. Federal laws not predicated on the receipt of federal funds would still apply and in some cases states have environmental regulations requiring their own environmental process.

States and Localities Would Have to Decide whether to Replace Revenues with State Taxes and What Types of Programs to Finance

States would have to decide whether to replace revenues with state taxes. This decision would have different impacts on different states because some states contribute more in taxes than they get back in program funds and vice versa. In the highway context, these states are referred to as donor and donee states. However, a turnback might require states to replace Highway Trust Fund revenues for transit programs and safety grants as well as highways. For some states replacing federal revenues with state taxes sufficient to continue to fund existing federal programs would result in a net decrease in fuel taxes in that state while in others a net increase in fuel taxes—in some cases a substantial increase. This raises questions whether surface transportation programs would continue at the same funding level under a turnback because states face their own long-term fiscal challenges, and the fiscal capacity of states varies. Other factors could affect outcomes at the state level. For example, there is no way to reliably predict the extent to which "tax competition" between states—efforts to keep taxes lower as a way of attracting business—would occur.

We considered the implications of a relatively complete turnback of federal grant programs, including highway, transit and safety grants. In the following example, almost all federal surface transportation programs funded through the Highway Trust Fund would be turned back to the states, with the exception of Federal Lands and Emergency Relief.[113] In order to provide a consistent basis for comparison, we assumed that states would substantially continue current programs and activities that now receive federal funding, and that states would raise their fuel taxes to provide the additional revenues needed to cover the cost of these programs and activities. However, if a turnback of the federal program were to actually occur, the outcome would almost certainly differ from these results, because states would not necessarily elect to replace all current federal programs or finance the same programs and activities from their own resources. Furthermore, states might not elect to replace federal revenue with state fuel taxes as states have options for raising revenue other than fuel taxes. For example, a state might choose to raise vehicle registration fees or increase the use of tolling.

The illustrative analysis of this turnback scenario showed that 27 states could achieve the same funding level as they currently receive through federal transportation grants with taxes lower than the existing federal tax, while 23 states and the District of Columbia would require taxes higher than the existing federal tax, or other revenue sources, to achieve full replacement value.

Figure 1 lists the net change in per-gallon fuel taxes that would occur if the federal fuel tax were eliminated and states replaced Highway Trust Fund grants with their own fuel taxes.[114] States in table 1 with a negative value would need to raise state taxes less than the current federal tax level, and states with a positive value would need to raise state taxes more than the current federal tax level, or obtain other revenue sources.

Although table 1 shows that a similar number of states would likely require net increases and net decreases, the range is much wider among states that would require a net increase. While some states, such as Virginia and Arizona, would likely end up with modest net decreases in fuel taxes of up to 6 cents per gallon under this scenario, nine states and the District of Columbia would face increases of more than twice that—Mississippi and Alaska would all require comparatively extreme net increases of more than 30 cents per gallon, and the District of Columbia over $1 per gallon. These results reflect a cumulative effect of many factors, such as the "donor-donee" distinctions between states, equity and minimum apportionment adjustments from the Highway Trust Fund, the various allocations made to states for safety, and allocations to states and localities for transit programs.

Table 1. Potential Fiscal Impact of Turning Back Federal Transportation Programs to the States, Assuming the Devolution of Almost All Programs and Revenues

	Net change in per-gallon tax rate If state replaced all federal funds using fuel tax (cents)		
State	**Highway account**	**Transit account**	**Total**
Virginia	-5.60	-0.44	**-6.04**
Arizona	-5.57	-0.47	**-6.04**
Kentucky	-3.57	-1.51	**-5.09**
Minnesota	-4.58	-0.47	**-5.05**
Ohio	-4.24	-0.41	**-4.64**
Colorado	-4.82	0.25	**-4.57**
Maine	-3.06	-1.45	**-4.52**
Tennessee	-3.22	-1.14	**-4.35**
Iowa	-2.91	-1.20	**-4.11**
Missouri	-3.00	-0.85	**-3.85**
Indiana	-2.82	-1.00	**-3.82**
Oregon	-3.67	0.29	**-3.38**
North Carolina	-1.97	-1.14	**-3.11**
Nevada	-2.91	-0.01	**-2.92**
Utah	-3.31	0.73	**-2.58**
Texas	-1.76	-0.78	**-2.53**
Georgia	-1.74	-0.73	**-2.48**

Table 1 (continued)			
South Carolina	-0.68	-1.75	**-2.43**
Wisconsin	-1.39	-0.68	**-2.08**
Michigan	-1.57	-0.40	**-1.96**
Oklahoma	-0.06	-1.73	**-1.79**
Pennsylvania	-3.98	2.26	**-1.71**
Nebraska	-0.42	-1.19	**-1.60**
New Hampshire	-0.05	-1.53	**-1.58**
Maryland	-3.84	2.26	**-1.58**
California	-3.62	2.11	**-1.51**
Alabama	1.04	-1.19	**-0.15**
New Mexico	1.18	-1.10	**0.08**
Florida	0.24	-0.07	**0.17**
Arkansas	1.82	-1.58	**0.24**
Kansas	1.65	-1.15	**0.50**
Illinois	-2.92	3.47	**0.55**
Washington	-0.69	2.07	**1.38**
New Jersey	-2.44	5.41	**2.96**
West Virginia	4.18	-0.66	**3.53**
Delaware	3.55	0.33	**3.88**
Wyoming	6.84	-1.79	**5.05**
Massachusetts	-0.37	5.76	**5.39**
Idaho	6.40	-0.68	**5.72**
Connecticut	4.03	4.17	**8.20**
Hawaii	3.57	5.12	**8.69**
North Dakota	14.31	-0.86	**13.46**
Vermont	14.39	-0.92	**13.47**
New York	1.77	12.53	**14.31**
South Dakota	14.94	-0.15	**14.78**
Louisiana	18.43	-0.77	**17.66**
Rhode Island	16.43	3.72	**20.15**
Montana	21.21	-0.48	**20.73**
Mississippi	32.75	-1.89	**30.86**
Alaska	40.32	8.61	**48.93**
District of Columbia	52.57	89.89	**142.46**

Source: GAO analysis of DOT data.

Notes: The Highway Account of the Highway Trust Fund receives 15.44 cents of the total 18.4 cents of the per-gallon federal gasoline tax; 21.44 cents of the total 24.4 cents of the federal diesel fuel tax goes to the Highway Account. The Transit

Account of the Highway Trust Fund receives 2.86 cents of the per-gallon federal gasoline tax.

States Would Have Flexibility in Funding Programs

In general, states would have great flexibility in how they use funds under a turnback approach. States would have greater flexibility to develop their own programs and approaches without being limited to the current federal program categories, and would have greater discretion to define and fund projects that best suit their needs. In addition, there would be no congressionally directed spending. To the extent that federal programs affect the targeting of funds, states might shift funds to different projects. However, the current federal-aid program already gives states great discretion in setting priorities and selecting projects. In contrast, the current federal program may provide some states with flexibility they otherwise would not have. For example, some federal highway programs provide that funds may be transferred (flexed) between highway and transit programs. However, under a turnback of surface transportation programs, this flexibility could be lost in some states. For example, some states have constitutional provisions that require all fuel taxes to be spent solely on roads, thus making transit and safety programs ineligible barring constitutional change. Such states would have to revise certain laws and constitutional provisions or develop alternative sources of revenue in order to replace federal funds.

Federal Roles and Goals

Surface Transportation: Preliminary Observations on Efforts to Restructure Current Program. GAO-08-478T. Washington, D.C.: February 6, 2008.

Freight Transportation: National Policy and Strategies Can Help Improve Freight Mobility. GAO-08-287. Washington, D.C.: January 7, 2008.

Highlights of a Forum: Transforming Transportation Policy for the 21st Century. GAO-07-1210SP. Washington, D.C.: September 19, 2007.

Railroad Bridges and Tunnels: Federal Role in Providing Safety Oversight and Freight Infrastructure Investment Could Be Better Targeted. GAO-07-770. Washington, D.C.: Aug. 6, 2007.

Motor Carrier Safety: Preliminary Information on the Federal Motor Carrier Safety Administration's Efforts to Identify and Follow Up with High-Risk Carriers. GAO-07-1074T. Washington, D.C.: July 11, 2007.

Intermodal Transportation: DOT Could Take Further Actions to Address Intermodal Barriers. GAO-07-718. Washington, D.C.: June 20, 2007.

Intercity Passenger Rail: National Policy and Strategies Needed to Maximize Public Benefits from Federal Expenditures. GAO-07-15. Washington, D.C.: November 13, 2006.

Freight Railroads: Industry Health Has Improved, but Concerns about Competition and Capacity Should Be Addressed. GAO-07-94. Washington, D.C.: October 6, 2006.

Public Transportation: New Starts Program Is in a Period of Transition. GAO-06-819. Washington, D.C.: August 30, 2006.

Freight Transportation: Short Sea Shipping Option Shows Importance of Systematic Approach to Public Investment Decisions. GAO-05-768. Washington, D.C.: July 29, 2005.

Rail Transit: Additional Federal Leadership Would Enhance FTA's State Safety Oversight Program. GAO-06-821. Washington, D.C.: July 26, 2006.

Intermodal Transportation: Potential Strategies Would Redefine Federal Role in Developing Airport Intermodal Capabilities. GAO-05-727. Washington, D.C.: July 26, 2005.

21st Century Challenges: Reexamining the Base of the Federal Government. GAO-05-325SP. Washington, D.C.: February, 2005.

Homeland Security: Effective Regional Coordination Can Enhance Emergency Preparedness. GAO-04-1009. Washington, D.C.: September 15, 2004.

Freight Transportation: Strategies Needed to Address Planning and Financing Limitations. GAO-04-165. Washington, D.C.: December 19, 2003.

Surface and Maritime Transportation: Developing Strategies for Enhancing Mobility: A National Challenge. GAO-02-775. Washington, D.C.: August 30, 2002.

Highway Infrastructure: Interstate Physical Conditions Have Improved, but Congestion and Other Pressures Continue. GAO-02-571. Washington, D.C.: May 31, 2002.

Performance and Accountability; Best Tools and Approaches

Highway Public-Private Partnerships: More Rigorous Up-front Analysis Could Better Secure Potential Benefits and Protect the Public Interest. GAO-08-44. Washington D.C.: February 8, 2008.

Federal-Aid Highways: Increased Reliance on Contractors Can Pose Oversight Challenges for Federal and State Officials. GAO-08-198. Washington D.C.: January 8, 2008.

A Call For Stewardship: Enhancing the Federal Government's Ability to Address Key Fiscal and Other 21st Century Challenges. GAO-08-93SP. Washington, D.C.: December 2007.

Public Transportation: Future Demand Is Likely for New Starts and Small Starts Programs, but Improvements Needed to the Small Starts Application Process. GAO-07-917. Washington, D.C.: July 27, 2007.

Surface Transportation: Strategies Are Available for Making Existing Road Infrastructure Perform Better. GAO-07-920. Washington, D.C.: July 26, 2007.

Motor Carrier Safety: A Statistical Approach Will Better Identify Commercial Carriers That Pose High Crash Risks Than Does the Current Federal Approach. GAO-07-585. Washington, D.C.: June 11, 2007.

Public Transportation: Preliminary Analysis of Changes to and Trends in FTA's New Starts and Small Starts Programs. GAO-07-812T. Washington, D.C.: May 10, 2007.

Older Driver Safety: Knowledge Sharing Should Help States Prepare for Increase in Older Driver Population. GAO-07-413. Washington, D.C.: April 11, 2007.

Older Driver Safety: Survey of States on Their Implementation of Federal Highway Administration Recommendations and Guidelines, an E-Supplement. GAO-07-517SP. Washington, D.C.: April 11, 2007.

Performance and Accountability: Transportation Challenges Facing Congress and the Department of Transportation. GAO-07-545T. Washington, D.C.: March 6, 2007.

Transportation-Disadvantaged Populations: Actions Needed to Clarify Responsibilities and Increase Preparedness for Evacuations. GAO-07-44. Washington, D.C.: December 22, 2006.

Federal Transit Administration: Progress Made in Implementing Changes to the Job Access Program, but Evaluation and Oversight Processes Need Improvement. GAO-07-43. Washington, D.C.: November 17, 2006.

Truck Safety: Share the Road Safely Pilot Initiative Showed Promise, but the Program's Future Success Is Uncertain. GAO-06-916. Washington, D.C.: September 8, 2006.

Public Transportation: Preliminary Information on FTA's Implementation of SAFETEA-LU Changes. GAO-06-910T. Washington, D.C.: June 27, 2006.

Intermodal Transportation: Challenges to and Potential Strategies for Developing Improved Intermodal Capabilities. GAO-06-855T. Washington, D.C.: June 15, 2006.

Federal Motor Carrier Safety Administration: Education and Outreach Programs Target Safety and Consumer Issues, but Gaps in Planning and Evaluation Remain. GAO-06-103. Washington, D.C.: December 19, 2005.

Large Truck Safety: Federal Enforcement Efforts Have Been Stronger Since 2000, but Oversight of State Grants Needs Improvement. GAO-06-156. Washington, D.C.: December 15, 2005.

Highway Safety: Further Opportunities Exist to Improve Data on Crashes Involving Commercial Motor Vehicles. GAO-06-102. Washington, D.C.: November 18, 2005.

Transportation Services: Better Dissemination and Oversight of DOT's Guidance Could Lead to Improved Access for Limited English-Proficient Populations. GAO-06-52. Washington, D.C.: November 2, 2005.

Highway Congestion: Intelligent Transportation Systems Promise for Managing Congestion Falls Short, and DOT Could Better Facilitate Their Strategic Use. GAO-05-943. Washington, D.C.: September 14, 2005.

Highlights of an Expert Panel: The Benefits and Costs of Highway and Transit Investments. GAO-05-423SP. Washington, D.C.: May 6, 2005.

Federal-Aid Highways: FHWA Needs a Comprehensive Approach to Improving Project Oversight. GAO-05-173. Washington, D.C.: January 31, 2005.

Highway and Transit Investments: Options for Improving Information on Projects' Benefits and Costs and Increasing Accountability for Results. GAO-05-172. Washington, D.C.: January 24, 2005.

Highway Safety: Improved Monitoring and Oversight of Traffic Safety Data Program Are Needed. GAO-05-24. Washington, D.C.: November 4, 2004.

Surface Transportation: Many Factors Affect Investment Decisions. GAO-04-744. Washington, D.C.: June 30, 2004.

Highway Safety: Better Guidance Could Improve Oversight of State Highway Safety Programs. GAO-03-474. Washington, D.C.: April 21, 2003.

Executive Guide: Leading Practices in Capital Decision Making. GAO/AIMD-99-32. Washington, D.C.: December 1998.

Fiscal Sustainability/ Financing the Nation's Transportation System

Congressional Directives: Selected Agencies' Processes for Responding to Funding Instructions. GAO-08-209. Washington, D.C.: January 31, 2008.

Highway and Transit Investments: Flexible Funding Supports State and Local Transportation Priorities and Multimodal Planning. GAO-07-772. Washington, D.C.: July 26, 2007.

State and Local Governments: Persistent Fiscal Challenges Will Likely Emerge within the Next Decade. GAO-07-1080SP. Washington D.C.: July 18, 2007.

Highway Emergency Relief: Reexamination Needed to Address Fiscal Imbalance and Long-Term Sustainability. GAO-07-245. Washington, D.C.: February 23, 2007.

High Risk Series: An Update. GAO-07-310. Washington, D.C.: January 2007.

Highway Finance: States' Expanding Use of Tolling Illustrates Diverse Challenges and Strategies. GAO-06-554. Washington, D.C.: June 28, 2006.

Highway Trust Fund: Overview of Highway Trust Fund Estimates. GAO-06-572T. Washington, D.C.: April 4, 2006.

Federal-Aid Highways: Trends, Effect on State Spending, and Options for Future Program Design. GAO-04-802. Washington, D.C.: August 31, 2004.

U.S. Infrastructure: Funding Trends and Federal Agencies' Investment Estimates. GAO-01-986T. Washington, D.C.: July 23, 2001.

Federal Budget: Choosing Public Investment Programs. GAO/AIMD-93-25. Washington, D.C.: July 23, 1993.

End Notes

[1] Additional information about GAO's simulations and the nation's long-term fiscal challenge can be found at http://www.gao.gov/special.pubs/longterm/.

[2] Formula grant programs allocate funds to states or their subdivisions in accordance with a distribution formula prescribed in law or administrative regulation. Grant recipients may then allocate these funds to specific projects based on program eligibility guidelines. Discretionary grant programs provide funds to recipients for specific projects or eligible activities based on eligibility and selection criteria as established by law, regulation, or on an administrative basis.

[3] Although federal funds are distributed to states through several individual grant programs, in aggregate, these grants are often referred to as a single federal program in each area of federal investment. For example, the collection of individual highway infrastructure grants

is commonly referred to as the Federal-Aid Highway program. Similarly, the assortment of federal motor carrier safety grants is collectively referred to as the federal motor carrier safety program.

[4] GAO, *Intercity Passenger Rail: National Policy and Strategies Needed to Maximize Public Benefits from Federal Expenditures*, GAO-07-15 (Washington, D.C.: Nov. 13, 2006).

[5] DOT defined congested conditions as periods of time where travel at less than free-flow speeds occurs on a portion of a road system.

[6] Transportation Research Board, *Critical Issues in Transportation* (Washington, D.C.: 2006).

[7] The HTF is divided into two major accounts, the Highway Account and the Mass Transit Account. A portion of federal fuel taxes is deposited into the Mass Transit Account. For example, of the 18.4 cents federal gas tax, 2.86 cents is deposited into the Mass Transit Account.

[8] CBO, *Public Spending on Transportation Infrastructure* (Washington, D.C.: Oct. 25, 2007).

[9] Congress created The National Surface Transportation Policy and Revenue Study Commission in 2005 under Section 1909 of the Safe, Accountable, Flexible, Efficient Transportation Equity Act—A Legacy for Users (SAFETEA-LU), Pub. L. No. 109-59, §1909, 119 Stat. 1471 (Aug. 10, 2005). The Commission was created to examine the condition and future needs of the nation's surface transportation system, and short and long-term alternatives to replace or supplement the fuel tax as the principal revenue source to support the HTF.

[10] Although federal transit funding was initially provided on a discretionary basis from the General Fund of the Treasury, highway user fees have replaced general revenues as the major source of transit assistance since the creation of the Mass Transit Account of the Highway Trust Fund by the Surface Transportation Assistance Act of 1982. Pub. L. No. 97-424, §531, 96 Stat. 2187 (Jan. 6, 1983).

[11] When federal operating assistance was initially established in 1974, large urbanized areas were eligible for these grants. However, operating assistance is currently limited to urbanized areas with a population of less than 200,000. See appendix II for more information about federal transit assistance programs.

[12] Pub. L. No. 87-866, §9, 76 Stat. 1148 (Oct. 23, 1962).

[13] Pub. L. No. 91-190, 83 Stat. 852 (Jan. 1, 1970); 42 USC §4321 et seq.

[14] Prior to the establishment of FMCSA by the Motor Carrier Safety Improvement Act of 1999, both FHWA and the former Interstate Commerce Commission (ICC) regulated separate aspects of motor carrier and commercial vehicle safety. When the ICC was terminated in 1995, its motor carrier and commercial vehicle regulatory authority was transferred to the Secretary of Transportation. Although some of the changes to the federal motor carrier programs and regulations predate FMCSA, for the purpose of clarity, we refer to FMCSA as the only modal administration with responsibility for motor carrier safety in the text. See app. II for more information about the history of federal motor carrier safety programs.

[15] On January 18, 2007, the President issued Executive Order 13422, "Amendment to Executive Order 12866 for Regulatory Planning and Review," which revised Executive Order 12866 to include a process for interagency coordination and review of significant guidance prior to issuance, among other procedural changes.

[16] The majority of highway infrastructure funding is distributed through seven major programs, often referred to as "core" highway programs. These programs are the National Highway System, Surface Transportation Program, Interstate Maintenance, Highway Bridge Replacement and Rehabilitation Program, Congestion Mitigation and Air Quality Improvement Program, Highway Safety Improvement Program, and the Equity Bonus Program. FHWA also administers a number of smaller, discretionary grants programs to provide federal highway infrastructure assistance to states.

[17] For most of the largest Federal-aid Highway programs, the minimum apportionment is 0.5 percent; each state must receive at least that much of the total money apportioned, regardless of other formula calculations.

[18] This also includes projects designated "high priority" by Congress in accordance with SAFETEA--LU.

[19] Based on state data, FHWA estimates how much tax revenue each state contributes to the Highway Trust Fund. The Equity Bonus Program guarantees states will receive a minimum rate of return on their contributions to the Highway Account of the Highway Trust Fund and a minimum funding increase relative to their average annual program apportionments under the previous transportation authorization bill, TEA-21, which authorized transportation programs from 1998–2003.

[20] Operating assistance is limited to urbanized areas with a population of less than 200,000.

[21] GAO is evaluating FTA's approach to measuring all of these factors, and identifying alternative approaches. GAO is planning to issue this report in July 2008.

[22] Transportation Research Board, *The Fuel Tax and Alternatives for Transportation Funding* (Washington, D.C.: 2006).

[23] In a process known as certification acceptance, states may certify that they will operate under state laws, regulations, directives, and standards at least equivalent to the current federal requirements.

[24] Interstate projects eligible for state oversight include resurfacing or other maintenance projects and new construction/reconstruction under $1 million.

[25] Federal planning requirements describe various tasks that state and local governments must perform and currently include developing strategic goals and objectives, considering a wide range of environmental and economic factors, preparing long-term and short-range plans, and ensuring an inclusive planning process.

[26] GAO, *Highlights of a Forum: Transforming Transportation Policy for the 21st Century*, GAO-07-1210SP (Washington, D.C.: September 2007).

[27] GAO, *Railroad Bridges and Tunnels: Federal Role in Providing Safety Oversight and Freight Infrastructure Investment Could Be Better Targeted*, GAO-07-770 (Washington, D.C.: Aug. 6, 2007).

[28] GAO, *Freight Transportation: Strategies Needed to Address Planning and Financing Limitations,* GAO-04-165 (Washington, D.C.: Dec. 19, 2003).

[29] The Freight Intermodal Distribution Pilot Grant Program is the only federal program specifically directed at intermodal infrastructure.

[30] GAO, *Intermodal Transportation: DOT Could Take Further Actions to Address Intermodal Barriers*, GAO-07-718 (Washington, D.C.: June 20, 2007).

[31] In part to address this problem, in 2006 DOT issued a request for applications for the new Corridors of the Future program, which will assist a limited number of multi-state partnerships selected through a competitive process.

[32] GAO-06-855T; GAO, *Intermodal Transportation: DOT Could Take Further Actions to Address Intermodal Barriers*, GAO-07-718 (Washington, D.C.: June 20, 2007); GAO, *Surface Transportation: Many Factors Affect Investment Decisions*, GAO-04-744 (Washington, D.C.: June 30, 2004); GAO-04-165.

[33] The FAST Corridor created an improved freight rail route and improved port access across several cities in Washington State, including Seattle and Tacoma.

[34] GAO-04-165.

[35] Transcript of New York City hearing of the National Surface Transportation Policy and Revenue Commission, Nov. 15, 2006.

[36] AASHTO, Vision for Metropolitan Transportation–Metropolitan Mobility and Congestion Issues Panel, March 19-20, 2007.

[37] Short sea shipping refers to moving freight on ships along coasts or on rivers; although it typically involves heavy or bulky cargoes that are not time-sensitive, in recent years there have been efforts to use it to transport cargo that would otherwise travel by truck or train.

[38] GAO, *Freight Transportation: Short Sea Shipping Option Shows Importance of Systematic Approach to Public Investment Decisions*, GAO-05-768 (Washington, D.C.: July 29, 2005).

[39] GAO, *High Risk Series: An Update*, GAO-07-310 (Washington, D.C.: Jan. 31, 2007); GAO, *Federal-Aid Highways: Trends, Effect on State Spending, and Options for Future Program Design*, GAO-04-802 (Washington, D.C.: Aug. 31, 2004).

[40] GAO, *Highway Infrastructure: Interstate Physical Conditions Have Improved, but Congestion and Other Pressures Continue*, GAO-02-571 (Washington, D.C.: May 31, 2002).

[41] *U.S. Department of Transportation Performance and Accountability Report for Fiscal Year 2007*, http://www.dot.gov/perfacc2007/index.htm; GAO-07-1210SP; GAO, *Performance and Accountability: Transportation Challenges Facing Congress and the Department of Transportation*, GAO-07-545T (Washington, D.C.: Mar. 6, 2007); GAO, *Federal-Aid Highways: FHWA Needs a Comprehensive Approach to Improving Project Oversight*, GAO-05-173 (Washington, D.C.: Jan. 31, 2005).

[42] FHWA program description, http://safety.fhwa.dot.gov/state_program/section402/402_over.htm.

[43] 49 CFR 350.327.

[44] GAO-07-545T.

45 The "equity bonus" criterion applies only in highway programs.

[46] FHWA Highway Statistics 2005 Table FA-4A, Apportionment Formulas: Federal-aid Highway Program, Enacted in SAFETEA-LU.

[47] GAO-07-545T.

[48] 23 U.S.C. 145.

[49] GAO-04-802.

[50] GAO, *Highway and Transit Investments: Flexible Funding Supports State and Local Transportation Priorities and Multimodal Planning*, GAO-07-772 (Washington, D.C.: July 26, 2007).

[51] GAO-04-802.

[52] Transfers to the highway program are permitted, but have been small compared to highway-to-transit transfers; only $40 million was moved from transit to highway programs between 1992 and 2002.

[53] GAO, *Highway Safety: Better Guidance Could Improve Oversight of State Highway Safety Programs,* GAO-03-474 (Washington, D.C.: Apr. 21, 2003).

[54] GAO, *Highway and Transit Investments: Options for Improving Information on Projects' Benefits and Costs and Increasing Accountability for Results*, GAO-05-172 (Washington, D.C.: Jan. 24, 2005).

[55] Federal Transit Administration, SAFETEA-LU: Authorization Levels for Fiscal Years 2005 Through 2009, http://www.fta.dot.gov/documents/SAFETEA-LU_Funding_by_Program_by_Year.pdf.

[56] GAO-05-172.

[57] GAO, *Surface Transportation: Strategies Are Available for Making Existing Road Infrastructure Perform Better*, GAO-07-920 (Washington, D.C.: July 26, 2007).

[58] GAO-07-920.

[59] GAO, *Freight Transportation: National Policy and Strategies Can Help Improve Freight Mobility*, GAO-08-287 (Washington, D.C.: Jan. 7, 2008); GAO-04-165.

[60] GAO-04-165.

[61] GAO-07-1210SP.

[62] AASHTO, Transportation – Invest in Our Future: A New Vision for the 21st Century, July 2007.

[63] Testimony of Thomas J. Madison Jr., Commissioner, New York State Department of Transportation, to the New York City hearing of the National Surface Transportation Policy and Revenue Study Commission, November 16, 2006.

[64] Congressional Research Service, *Surface Transportation Congestion: Policy and Issues* (RL 33995) May 10, 2007; GAO-07-770.

[65] GAO, *Rail Transit: Additional Federal Leadership Would Enhance FTA's State Safety Oversight Program*, GAO-06-821 (Washington, D.C.: July 26, 2006).

[66] GAO, *Highway Safety: Improved Monitoring and Oversight of Traffic Safety Data Program Are Needed,* GAO-05-24 (Washington, D.C.: Nov. 4, 2004).

[67] Under congestion pricing, toll rates vary with demand. ITS employs technologies such as monitoring of traffic conditions and optimized timing of traffic signals.

[68] GAO-07-920; GAO, *Highway Congestion: Intelligent Transportation Systems' Promise for Managing Congestion Falls Short, and DOT Could Better Facilitate Their Strategic Use,* GAO-05-943 (Washington, D.C.: Sept. 14, 2005).

[69] GAO-05-943.

[70] GAO-04-802.

[71] In our analysis, as well as the other studies that we reviewed, the focus was on highway spending. Thus, if increased federal grants for highways led states and localities to shift their own funds from highway spending to transit spending, such a shift would be considered substitution. To the extent that occurred, then the substitution away from total transportation spending from increased federal grants would be smaller than the rates that we and others estimated.

[72] In contrast, for the New Starts transit capital program, the level of state and local contributions is a factor the FTA considers in awarding discretionary grants.

[73] Projects of National and Regional Significance was created as part of SAFETEA-LU to provide funding for high cost projects of national or regional importance that have total costs higher than $500 million or higher than 75 percent of the state's annual federal highway funds. Although it was established in law as a competitive program, the competition never took place because Congress directed all the funds to specific projects.

[74] GAO, *Congressional Directives: Selected Agencies' Processes for Responding to Funding Instructions*, GAO-08-209 (Washington, D.C.: Jan. 31, 2008).

[75] CBO, *Status of the Highway Trust Fund: 2007* (Washington, D.C.: Mar. 27, 2007).

[76] The unexpended balance in the Highway Account of the Highway Trust Fund grew from about $10 billion in 1995 to about $23 billion in 2000, according to the CBO.

[77] GAO-07-310.

[78] The most recent major restructuring of federal surface transportation policy occurred in 1991, with the passage of the Intermodal Surface Transportation Efficiency Act (ISTEA), which consolidated highway grant categories and substantially increased transfer flexibility between highway and transit funds.

[79] The Equity Bonus Program provides the most funding to states on an annual basis. However, rather than providing funds directly to states for allocation to eligible projects like other highway programs, the Equity Bonus Program distributes funds to states through the other core highway programs.

[80] GAO, *Homeland Security: Effective Regional Coordination Can Enhance Emergency Preparedness*, GAO-04-1009 (Washington, D.C.: Sept. 15, 2004).

[81] Public Sector Comparators are a quantitative analysis technique used to compare the cost of completing a project using public versus public-private partnership delivery methods. Value-for-Money analyses are often completed as part of that process, and calculate total project benefits and costs; they are not limited to financial aspects, and often examine factors that are hard to quantify, such as the quality of construction. For further discussion, see GAO, *Highway Public-Private Partnerships: More Rigorous Up-front Analysis Could Better Secure Potential Benefits and Protect the Public Interest*, GAO-08-44 (Washington D.C.: Feb. 8, 2008).

[82] GAO-07-1210SP.

[83] Only the lightest combination unit vehicles pay sufficient taxes and fees to cover the costs they impose on highways.

[84] GAO, *Freight Railroads: Industry Health Has Improved, but Concerns about Competition and Capacity Should Be Addressed*, GAO-07-94 (Washington, D.C.: Oct. 6, 2006).

[85] GAO, *Highway Public-Private Partnerships: More Rigorous Up-Front Analysis Could Better Secure Potential Benefits and Protect the Public Interest*, GAO-08-44 (Washington, D.C.: Feb. 8, 2008).

[86] GAO, *21st Century Challenges: Reexamining the Base of the Federal Government*, GAO-05-325SP (Washington, D.C.: Feb. 1, 2005).

[87] National Surface Transportation Policy and Revenue Study Commission, *Transportation for Tomorrow* (Washington, D.C.: Jan. 15, 2008).

[88] FHWA also conducts research activities at the Turner-Fairbank Highway Research Center. These activities are coordinated by FHWA's Office of Research, Development, and Technology.

[89] Pub. L. No. 102-240 (Dec. 18, 1991).

[90] This number includes division offices in Puerto Rico and the District of Columbia, as well as FLH division offices in Lakewood, Colo.; Sterling, Va.; and Vancouver, Wash.

[91] The Highway Trust Fund is divided into two major accounts, the Highway Account and the Mass Transit Account. A portion of federal fuel taxes is deposited into the Mass Transit Account. For example, of the 18.4 cents federal gas tax, 2.86 cents is deposited into the Mass Transit Account.

[92] Operating assistance is limited to urbanized areas with a population of less than 200,000.

[93] Some programs such as the Formula Grant Program for Other Than Urbanized Areas provide a greater federal share of funding if states have a high percentage of federal lands. This program also provides a higher federal match for projects that meet requirements of the American Disabilities Act, the Clean Air Act, or bicycle access projects. Lower federal matches include capital assistance from the Over the Road Bus Accessibility Program and federal assistance for operating expenses under the Formula Grant Program for Other Than Urbanized Areas and Urbanized Area Formula Grants, which are capped at 50 percent.

[94] The Over-the-Road Bus Accessibility Program also awards funds on a national competitive basis to help finance incremental capital and training costs associated with DOT's regulations on transit accessibility for disabled and special needs populations in rural areas.

[95] Full federal oversight refers to federal oversight at the project level.

[96] For program management process reviews, FTA officials or contractors review grant recipients' management systems and records to ensure recipients are adhering to statutory and administrative requirements such as federal planning, civil rights, and other provisions. FTA's project management reviews require federal oversight at the project rather than program level. Areas of review include grantee recipient's fiscal and management capacity to implement the project, project progress according to planned specifications, schedule, and budget levels, among others.

[97] FTA also conducts reviews in specialized areas such as financial management, procurement, civil rights, and planning processes, among others.

[98] Pub. L. No. 88-365, §10, 78 Stat. 307 (July 9, 1964).

[99] Pub. L. No. 95-599, § 313, 92 Stat. 2748 (Nov. 6, 1978) and Pub. L. No. 95-599, §323, 92 Stat. 2754 (Nov. 6, 1978).

[100] Pub. L. No. 91-453, §16, 84 Stat. 967 (Oct. 15, 1970).

[101] Pub. L. No.105-178, § 3037, 112 Stat. 387 (June 9, 1998).

[102] Pub. L. No. 109-59, §3021, 119 Stat. 1608 (Aug. 10, 2005).

[103] NHTSA administers four grant programs that do not target specific accident factors. These include grants to prohibit racial profiling, and grants for innovative approaches to highway safety, state traffic safety systems, and highway safety research activities.

[104] This program also sets aside funds for grants to the 10 states with the highest impaired-driving fatality rates.

[105] Although highway infrastructure funds are transferred to states' Section 402 program funds, states may allocate transferred funds back to the Federal-Aid Highway Program for use on safety-related infrastructure improvements.

[106] MCSAP basic grants also require states to maintain their average previous expenditure levels for commercial motor vehicle safety and traffic safety enforcement programs.

[107] Some motor carrier safety grants such as State Safety Data Improvement grants and CVISN Core Deployment grants have statutorily-defined criteria. For example, State Safety Data Improvement grants criteria include: conducting a comprehensive audit of data systems within the past 2 years, developing a plan that identifies and prioritizes safety data needs and goals, and identifying performance measures to track progress toward those goals.

[108] A notable exception is the 55 mph speed limit enforcement spending provision, which was established first as an incentive/penalty grant in 1978 and then changed to a mandatory spending restriction on Section 402 funds in 1982 until its repeal in 1995.

[109] Advisory Commission on Intergovernmental Relations, *Devolving Selected Federal-Aid Highway Programs and Revenue Bases: A Critical Appraisal* (Washington, D.C.: September 1987).

[110] Program was created as the Disaster Relief Act of 1974, Pub. L. No. 93-288, 88 Stat. 143, May 22, 1974, and was later amended and renamed in 2000 by Pub. L. No. 106-390 §301, 114 Stat. 1572, Oct. 30, 2000; 42 U.S.C. § 5121 et seq.

[111] GAO, *Federal-Aid Highways: Increased Reliance on Contractors Can Pose Oversight Challenges for Federal and State Officials*, GAO-08-198 (Washington, D.C.: Jan. 8, 2008).

[112] 49 CFR Part 26.

[113] Many different variations of a turnback approach could be posited, including ones that retain some federal programs and some level of federal gasoline tax. These scenarios would yield different results. This analysis illustrates the potential fiscal impact of turnback by providing a common basis for comparing the state tax burden that would be necessary to maintain the same level of revenue in the absence of a federal grant program.

[114] There are methodological limitations to this analysis. These results represent only 1 year of federal surface transportation programs, and shifts in fuel usage and other factors cause change from year to year. Sampling multiple years was not practical because the changeover from the TEA-21 authorization to the SAFETEA-LU authorization resulted in grant disbursement and fuel consumption data that are not equivalent across years. Also, discretionary programs were omitted because their grants typically last for only 1 or several years, and they represent a small portion federal grant funds. Finally, because this analysis only considers programs funded by the federal fuel tax via the Highway Trust Fund, the few programs financed from general funds—most notably the New Starts transit capital grant program—are outside the scope of analysis.

In: Surface Transportation ISBN: 978-1-60692-357-3
Editor: Keith A. Libermann, PP: 81-111

Chapter 2

SURFACE TRANSPORTATION: PRINCIPLES CAN GUIDE EFFORTS TO RESTRUCTURE AND FUND FEDERAL PROGRAMS

Government Accountability Office

WHY GAO DID THIS STUDY

The nation has reached a critical juncture with its current surface transportation policies and programs. Demand has outpaced the capacity of the system, resulting in increased congestion. In addition, without significant changes in funding levels or planned spending, the Highway Trust Fund—the major source of federal highway and transit funding— is projected to incur significant deficits in the years ahead. Exacerbating concerns about the solvency of the Highway Trust Fund is the federal government's bleak fiscal condition and outlook. As a result, other federal revenue sources may not be available to help solve the nation's current transportation challenges.

This statement is based on a body of work that GAO has completed over the past several years for Congress. This testimony discusses (1) GAO's recent findings on the structure and performance of the current surface transportation program (GAO-08-400), (2) a framework to assess proposals for restructuring of the surface transportation program, (3) potential options to fund investments in the surface transportation system, and (4) our recent findings on the benefits, costs, and trade-offs of using public-private partnerships to help fund transportation investments (GAO-08-44).

WHAT GAO FOUND

Since federal fundingfor the interstate system was established in 1956, the federal role in surface transportation has expanded to include broader goals, more programs, and a variety of program structures. Consequently, the goals of current programs are numerous and sometimes conflicting, and the federal role in these programs is unclear. For example, federal programs do not effectively address key transportation challenges, such as increasing congestion and freight demand. Many surface transportation programs are also not linked to performance of the transportation system or of the grantees, and programs often do not employ the best tools and approaches. Finally, the fiscal sustainability of the numerous highway, transit, and safety programs funded by the Highway Trust Fund is in doubt, because spending from the fund has increased without commensurate increases in revenues.

A number of principles can help guide the assessment of proposals to restructure and fund federal surface transportation programs. These principles include (1) ensuring goals are well defined and focused on the national interest, (2) ensuring the federal role in achieving each goal is clearly defined, (3) ensuring accountability for results by entities receiving federal funds, (4) employing the best tools and approaches to improve results and emphasize return on targeted federal investment, and (5) ensuring fiscal sustainability.

A range of options could be used to fund the growing demand for additional investment in the surface transportation system. There are two revenue sources for these additional investments: taxes and fees. Financing mechanisms, such as bonding and revolving funds, could also be used to fund transportation infrastructure projects when tax and user fee approaches are not sufficient to meet demands. However, these financing mechanisms are all forms of debt that ultimately must be repaid with interest by the general population through tax increases or reductions in government services. Each of these options has different merits and challenges, and the selection of any of them will likely involve trade-offs among different policy goals.

Highway public-private partnerships show promise as a viable alternative, where appropriate, to help meet growing and costly transportation demands. The highway public-private partnerships created to date have resulted in advantages from the perspective of state and local governments, such as the construction of new infrastructure without using public funding. However, highway public-private partnerships also entail potential costs and risks including the reality that funds from public-private partnerships are largely a new source of borrowed funds—a form of privately issued debt that must be repaid to private investors. Ultimately the extent to which public-private partnerships can be used to help meet the nation's transportation funding challenges will depend on the ability of states to weigh potential benefits against potential costs and trade-offs to determine whether public-private partnerships are appropriate in specific circumstances—and if so—how best to implement them and protect the public interest.

July 10, 2008

Mr. Chairman and Members of the Committee:

We appreciate the opportunity to testify on surface transportation financing issues. As you know, the nation has reached a critical juncture with current surface transportation programs. The current federal approach to addressing the nation's surface transportation problems is not working well. Despite large increases in expenditures in real terms for transportation, the investment has not commensurately improved the performance of the nation's surface transportation system, as congestion continues to grow and looming problems from the anticipated growth in travel demand are not being adequately addressed. The economic and environmental implications are significant, ranging from wasted fuel and lost time as cars idle in traffic to increased costs for businesses as the transportation system grows more unreliable.

Since federal funding for the interstate system was established in 1956, the federal role in surface transportation has expanded to include broader goals, more programs, and a variety of program structures. However, many of these programs do not effectively address key transportation challenges, such as increasing congestion and freight demand, because the federal goals and roles of the programs are unclear, the programs are generally not need or performance-based, and the programs often do not employ the best tools or approaches. In addition, the continued relevance of some of these programs in the 21st century is unclear. For example, the Highway Trust Fund was created in 1956 to distribute funds for the construction of the interstate highway system. That system is now complete. However, the federal highway program's funding and delivery mechanisms have not substantially changed. Furthermore, there is a growing differential between expected Highway Trust Fund revenue and planned levels of spending on surface transportation programs. As a result, without significant changes in funding levels or planned spending, the Highway Trust Fund is projected to incur significant deficits in the years ahead. As a result, in 2007, we added financing the nation's transportation system to GAO's High Risk List.[1]

Addressing these challenges is complicated by the breadth of the nation's surface transportation network—encompassing highway, transit, and rail systems and ports that are owned, funded, and operated by both the public and the private sectors. Moreover, surface transportation policy decisions are inextricably linked with aviation, economic, environmental, and energy policy concerns. In addition, exacerbating this challenge is that the federal government's financial condition and fiscal outlook are worse than many may understand.[2] Specifically, the federal budget is on an unsustainable path—heightening concern about the solvency of the Highway Trust Fund because other federal revenue sources may not be available to help solve the nation's current transportation challenges. Addressing these challenges requires strategic and intermodal approaches, effective tools and programs, and coordinated solutions involving all levels of government and the private sector. Yet in many cases, the government is still trying to do business in ways that are based on conditions, priorities, and approaches that were established decades ago and are not well suited to addressing 21st century challenges. Consequently, we have called for a fundamental reexamination of the nation's transportation policies and programs.[3]

Prudent use of taxpayer dollars is always important. The economic and social importance of the nation's transportation system and the current fiscal environment, make it even more important that federal, state, and local governments make prudent decisions on how to invest limited available resources. In making these decisions, governments will face an array of challenges that include repairing and maintaining aging infrastructure, making more efficient use of existing infrastructure, accounting for population growth, and incorporating new technologies in funding for infrastructure. In this environment, the infrastructure improvements that all levels of government want may not reflect what they need or what the nation can afford. Accordingly, decisions about the appropriate level of spending and distribution on infrastructure are both difficult and enormously important.

My remarks today focus on (1) our recent findings on the structure and performance of current surface transportation programs, (2) a framework to assess proposals for restructuring surface transportation programs, (3) potential options to fund investments in the surface transportation system, and (4) our recent findings on the benefits, costs, and trade-offs of using public-private partnerships to help fund transportation investments. My comments are based on a body of work that we have completed over the past several years for Congress.[4] We conducted our work in June 2008 in accordance with generally accepted government auditing standards. Those standards require that we plan and perform the audit to obtain sufficient, appropriate evidence to provide a reasonable basis for our findings and conclusions based on our audit objectives. We believe that the evidence obtained provides a reasonable basis for our findings and conclusions based on our audit objectives.

SUMMARY

Current surface transportation programs do not effectively address the transportation challenges the nation faces. Collectively, post-interstate-era programs addressing highway, transit, and safety are an agglomeration that has been established over half a century without a well-defined vision of the national interest and federal role. For example, federal programs do not effectively address key transportation challenges, such as increasing highway congestion and freight demand. Many surface transportation programs are not linked to the performance of the transportation system or of the grantees, and the programs often do not use the best tools or best approaches. Moreover, the fiscal sustainability of the numerous highway, transit, and safety programs funded by the Highway Trust Fund is in doubt.

Through our prior analysis of surface transportation programs, we have identified a framework of principles that can help inform Congress in assessing various proposals for restructuring and funding federal surface transportation programs. These principles are

- creating well-defined goals based on identified areas of national interest, which involves examining the relevance and relative priority of existing programs in light of 21st century challenges and identifying emerging areas of national importance;
- establishing and clearly defining the federal role in achieving each goal in relation to the roles of state and local governments, regional entities, and the private sector;
- incorporating performance and accountability into funding decisions to ensure resources are targeted to programs that best achieve intended outcomes and national priorities;
- employing the best tools, such as benefit-cost analysis, and approaches to emphasize return on investment at a time of constrained federal resources; and

- ensuring fiscal sustainability through targeted investments of federal, state, local, and private resources.

A range of options could be used to fund the demand for additional investment in the surface transportation system. Although some of the demand for additional investment in transportation could be reduced by, for example, using the existing infrastructure more efficiently, there is a growing consensus that some level of additional investment in transportation could be warranted. There are two revenue sources for these additional investments: taxes and fees. A variety of taxes have been and could be used to fund the nation's infrastructure, including excise, sales, property, and income taxes. Additionally, user fees such as fees based on vehicle miles traveled, freight container fees, customs duties, or congestion pricing of roads could be used. Financing mechanisms could also be used to fund transportation infrastructure projects when tax and user fee approaches are not sufficient to meet demands. However, these financing approaches, including bonding strategies, loans, loan guarantees, and revolving funds, are all forms of debt that ultimately must be repaid with interest by the general population through tax increases or reductions in government services.

Highway public-private partnerships also show promise as a viable alternative, where appropriate, to help meet growing and costly transportation demands. The highway public-private partnerships created to date have resulted in advantages from the perspective of state and local governments, such as the construction of new infrastructure without using public funding, and obtaining funds by extracting value from existing facilities for reinvestment in transportation and other public programs. However, highway public-private partnerships also entail potential costs and risks. Most importantly, there is no "free" money in public-private partnerships. While highway public-private partnerships can be used to obtain financing for highways, these funds are largely a new source of borrowed funds—a form of privately issued debt that must be repaid to private investors seeking a return on their investment by road users over what potentially could be a period of several generations. Ultimately the extent to which public-private partnerships can be used to help meet the nation's transportation funding challenges will depend on the ability of states to weigh potential benefits against potential costs and trade-offs to determine whether public-private partnerships are appropriate in specific circumstances—and if so—how best to implement them and protect the public interest. As we recently reported, consideration of public-private partnerships in the United States could benefit from more consistent, rigorous, systematic, up-front analysis and fresh thinking about the appropriate federal approach.[5] Reexamining the federal role in transportation provides an opportunity to identify the emerging national public interests in highway public-private partnerships and to determine how highway public-private partnerships fit in with national programs.

CURRENT SURFACE TRANSPORTATION PROGRAMS DO NOT EFFECTIVELY ADDRESS IDENTIFIED TRANSPORTATION CHALLENGES

Current surface transportation programs do not effectively address the transportation challenges the nation faces. Collectively, post-interstate-era programs addressing highway, transit, and safety are an agglomeration that has been established over half a century without a well-defined vision of the national interest and federal role. Many surface transportation programs are not linked to performance of the transportation system or grantees, as most highway, transit, and safety funds are distributed through formulas that only indirectly relate to needs and may have no relationship to performance. In addition, the programs often do not use the best tools or best approaches, such as using more rigorous economic analysis to select projects. Finally, the fiscal sustainability of the numerous highway, transit, and safety programs funded by the Highway Trust Fund is in doubt, as a result of increased spending from the fund without commensurate increases in revenues.

Federal Goals and Approaches Have Expanded as State and Local Discretion Has Increased

Since the Federal-Aid Highway Act of 1956 funded the modern federal highway program, the federal role in surface transportation has expanded to include broader goals, more programs, and a variety of program structures. Although most surface transportation funds remain dedicated to highway infrastructure, federal surface transportation programs have grown in number and complexity, incorporating additional transportation, environmental, and societal goals. While some of these goals have led to new grant programs in areas such as transit, highway safety, and motor carrier safety, others have led to additional procedural requirements for receiving federal aid, such as environmental review and transportation planning requirements.

This expansion has also created a variety of grant structures and federal approaches for establishing priorities and distributing federal funds. Most highway infrastructure funds continue to be distributed to states in accordance with individual grant program formulas and eligibility requirements. However, broad program goals, eligibility requirements, and authority to transfer funds between highway programs give state and local governments broad discretion to allocate highway infrastructure funds according to their priorities. Although some transit formula grant programs also give grantees considerable discretion to allocate funds, a portion of transit assistance requires grantees to compete for funding based on specific criteria and goals. Similarly, basic safety formula grant programs are augmented by smaller programs that directly target federal funds to specific goals and actions using financial incentives and penalty provisions.

The Goals and Role of the Federal Government Are Not Clear, and Many Programs Are Not Linked to Performance

We have found that many federal surface transportation programs are not effective at addressing key transportation challenges, such as increasing congestion and growing freight demand, because federal goals and roles are unclear, and many programs lack links to needs or performance. The goals of federal surface transportation programs are numerous and sometimes conflicting, which contributes to a corresponding lack of clarity in the federal role. For example, despite statutes and regulations that call for an intermodal approach (one that creates connections across modes), only one federal program is specifically directed at intermodal infrastructure.

Most highway, transit, and safety grant funds are distributed through formulas that have only an indirect relationship to needs and many have no relationship to performance or outcomes. The largest safety grants are more likely than highway grants to be focused on goals rather than specific transportation systems such as the interstate system, and several highway safety and motor carrier safety grants allocate incentive funds on the basis of performance or state efforts to carry out specific safety-related activities. However, since the majority of surface transportation funds are distributed without regard to performance, it is difficult to assess the impact of recent record levels of federal highway expenditures. For example, while the condition of highways showed some improvement between 1997 and 2004, traffic congestion increased in the same period. Mechanisms to link programs to goals also appear insufficient because, particularly within the Federal-aid Highway program, federal rules for transferring funds between different highway infrastructure programs are flexible, weakening the distinctions between individual programs (see Figure 1).

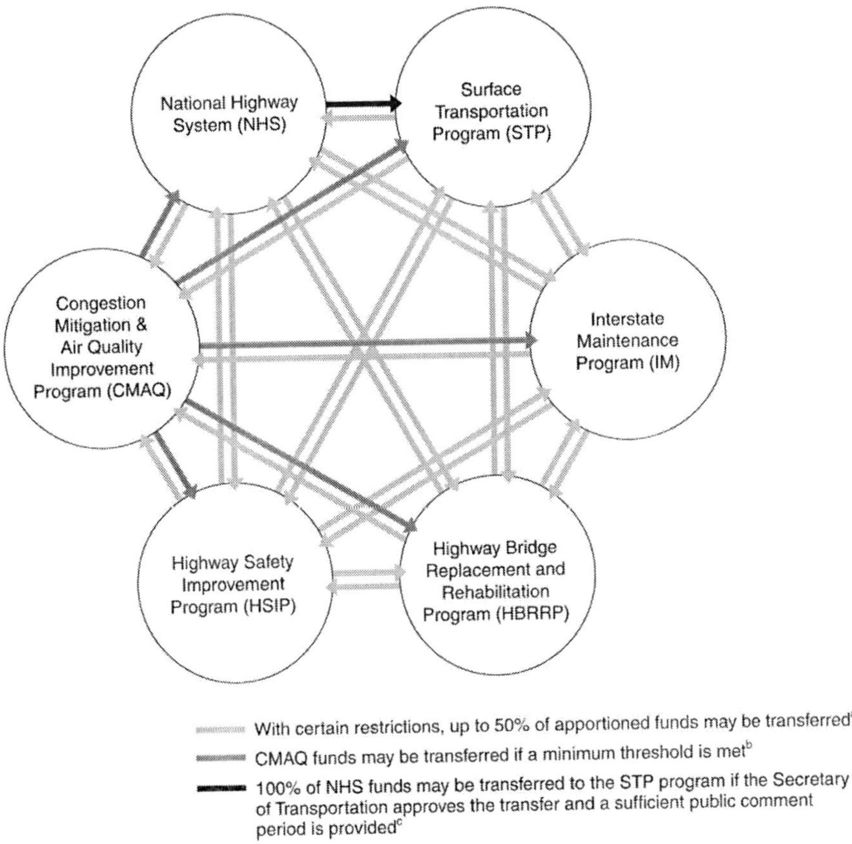

Source: GAO.

Figure 1. Broad Flexible Fund Transfer Provisions within Highway Programs.

Surface Transportation Programs Often Do Not Use Best Tools and Approaches

Surface transportation programs often do not employ the best tools and approaches to ensure effective investment decisions. Rigorous economic analysis does not generally drive the investment decisions of state and local governments—in a 2004 survey of state departments of transportation, 34 of 43 state departments of transportation cited political support and public opinion as very important factors, whereas 8 said the same of the ratio of benefits to costs.[6] The federal government also does not possess adequate data to assess outcomes or implement performance measures. For example, the Department of Transportation (DOT) does not have a central source of data on congestion, even though it has identified congestion as a top priority. While some funds can be transferred between highway and transit programs, modally stovepiped funding nevertheless impedes efficient planning and project selection. Additionally, tools to make better use of existing infrastructure, such as intelligent transportation systems and congestion pricing, have not been deployed to their full potential.

The Fiscal Sustainability of Surface Transportation Programs Is Threatened

The solvency of the federal surface transportation program is at risk because expenditures now exceed revenues for the Highway Trust Fund, and projections indicate that the balance of the Highway Trust Fund will soon be exhausted. According to the Congressional Budget Office (CBO), the Highway Account will face a shortfall in 2009, the Transit Account in 2012.[7] The rate of expenditures has affected its fiscal sustainability. As a result of the Transportation Equity Act for the 21st Century (TEA-21), Highway Trust Fund spending rose 40 percent from 1999 to 2003 and averaged $36.3 billion in contract authority per year. The upward trend in expenditures continued under the Safe, Accountable, Flexible, Efficient Transportation Equity Act: A Legacy for Users (SAFETEA-LU), which provided an average of $57.2 billion in contract authority per year. While expenditures from the trust fund have grown, revenues into the fund have not kept pace. The current fuel tax of 18.4 cents per gallon has been in place since 1993, and the buying power of the fixed cents-per-gallon amount has since been eroded by inflation. The reallocation to the Highway Trust Fund of 4.3 cents of federal fuel tax previously dedicated to deficit reduction provided an influx of funds beginning in 1997. However, this influx has been insufficient to sustain current spending levels.

Furthermore, while federal funding for transportation has increased, the total funding for transportation may not increase to the same extent because federal funds may be substituted for state and local funds. Thus, added federal funds may not lead to a commensurate increase in the total investment in highways because state and local governments can shift nonfederal funds away from highways to other purposes. Increases in federal funding do appear to reduce state spending for the same purpose, reducing the return on the federal investment. Research estimates that about 50 percent of each additional federal grant dollar for the highway program displaces funds that states would otherwise have spent on highways.

As we have previously reported, this situation argues for a fundamental reexamination of the federal approach to surface transportation problems and a restructuring of federal programs to create more focused, performance-based, and sustainable programs.[8] In cases for which there is a significant national interest, maintaining strong federal financial support and a more direct federal involvement in the program may be needed. In other cases, functions may best be carried out by other levels of government or not at all. There may also be cases for which federal financial support is desirable but a more results-oriented approach is appropriate. In addition, depending on the transportation issue and the desired goals, different options and approaches may be appropriate for different problems. Restructuring the current approach to transportation problems will take time, but a vision and strategy are needed to begin the process of transforming to a set of policies and programs to effectively address the nation's transportation needs and priorities.

Framework to Assess Proposals for Restructuring and Funding Surface Transportation Programs

Through our prior analyses of existing programs, we identified a framework of principles that could help drive an assessment of proposals for restructuring and funding federal surface transportation programs. These principles include (1) creating well-defined goals based on identified areas of national interest, (2) establishing and clearly defining the federal role in achieving each goal, (3) incorporating performance and accountability into funding decisions, (4) employing the best tools and approaches to improve results and emphasize return on investment, and (5) ensuring fiscal sustainability. We have also developed a series of illustrative questions that can be used to determine the extent to which restructuring and funding proposals are aligned with each principle. We developed these principles and illustrative questions based on prior analyses of existing surface transportation programs as well as a body of work that we have developed for Congress, including GAO's High-Risk, Performance and Accountability, and 21st Century Challenges reports. The principles do not prescribe a specific approach to restructuring or funding, but they do provide key attributes that will help ensure that restructured surface transportation programs address current challenges.

Create Well-defined Goals Based on Identified Areas of National Interest

Our previous work has shown that identifying areas of national interest is an important first step in any proposal to restructure and fund surface transportation programs. In identifying areas of national interest, proposals should consider existing 21st century challenges and how future trends could affect emerging areas of national importance—as well as how the national interest and federal role may vary by area. For example, experts have suggested that federal transportation policy should recognize emerging national and global imperatives, such as reducing the nation's dependence on oil and minimizing the impact of the transportation system on global climate change. Once the various national interests in surface transportation have been identified, proposals should also clarify specific goals for federal involvement in surface transportation programs. Goals should be specific and outcome-based to ensure that resources are targeted to projects that further the national interest.

The following illustrative questions can be used to determine the extent to which proposals to restructure and fund surface transportation programs create well-defined goals based on identified areas of national interest.

- To what extent are areas of national interest clearly defined?
- To what extent are areas of national interest reflective of future trends?

- To what extent are goals defined in relation to identified areas of national interest?

Establish and Clearly Define the Federal Role in Achieving Each Goal

After the various national interests and specific goals for federal involvement in surface transportation have been identified, the federal role in working toward each goal should be established. The federal role should be defined in relation to the roles of state and local governments, regional entities, and the private sector. Where the national interest is greatest, the federal government may play a more direct role in setting priorities and allocating resources as well as fund a higher share of program costs. Conversely, where the national interest is less evident, state and local governments and others could assume more responsibility. For example, efforts to reduce transportation's impact on greenhouse gas emissions may warrant a greater federal role than other initiatives, such as reducing urban congestion, since the impacts of greenhouse gas emissions are widely dispersed, whereas the impacts of urban congestion may be more localized.

The following illustrative questions can be used to determine the extent to which proposals to restructure and fund the surface transportation programs establish and clearly define the federal role in achieving each goal.

- To what extent is the federal role directly linked to defined areas of national interest and goals?
- To what extent is the federal role defined in relation to the roles of state and local governments, regional entities, and the private sector?
- To what extent does the proposal consider how the transportation system is linked to other sectors and national policies, such as environmental, security, and energy policies?

Incorporate Performance and Accountability into Funding Decisions

Our previous work has shown that an increased focus on performance and accountability for results could help the federal government target resources to programs that best achieve intended outcomes and national transportation priorities. Tracking specific outcomes that are clearly linked to program goals could provide a strong foundation for holding grant recipients responsible for achieving federal objectives and measuring overall program performance. In particular, substituting specific performance measures for the current federal procedural requirements could help make the program more outcome-oriented. For example, if reducing congestion were an established federal goal, outcome measures for congestion, such as reduced travel time, could be incorporated into the programs to hold state and local governments responsible for meeting specific performance targets. Furthermore, directly linking the allocation of resources to the program outcomes would increase the focus on performance and accountability for results. Incorporating incentives or penalty provisions into grants can further hold grantees and recipients accountable for achieving results.

The following illustrative questions can be used to determine the extent to which proposals to restructure and fund surface transportation programs incorporate performance and accountability into funding decisions.

- Are national performance goals identified and discussed in relation to state, regional, and local performance goals?
- To what extent are performance measures outcome-based?
- To what extent is funding linked to performance?
- To what extent does the proposal include provisions for holding stakeholders accountable for achieving results?

Employ the Best Tools and Approaches to Improve Results and Emphasize Return on Investment

We have previously reported that the effectiveness of any overall federal program design can be increased by promoting and facilitating the use of the best tools and approaches to improve results and emphasize return on investment. Importantly, given the projected growth in federal deficits, constrained state and local budgets, and looming Social Security and Medicare spending commitments, the resources available for discretionary programs will be more limited—making it imperative to maximize the national public benefits of any federal investment through a rigorous examination of the use of such funds.[9] A number of specific tools and approaches can be used to improve results and return on investment including using economic analysis, such as benefit-cost analysis, in project selection; requiring grantees to conduct post-project evaluations; creating incentives to better utilize existing infrastructure; providing states and localities with greater flexibility to use certain tools, such as tolling and congestion pricing; and requiring maintenance-of-effort provisions in grants. Using these tools and approaches could help surface transportation programs more directly address national transportation priorities.

The following illustrative questions can be used to determine the extent to which proposals to restructure and fund surface transportation programs employ the best tools and approaches to improve results and emphasize return on investment.

- To what extent do the proposals consider how costs and revenues will be shared among federal, state, local, and private stakeholders?
- To what extent do the proposals address the need better to align fees and taxes with use and benefits?
- To what extent are trade-offs between efficiency and equity considered?
- Do the tools and approaches align with the level of federal involvement in a given policy area?
- To what extent do the proposals provide flexibility and incentives for state and local governments to choose the most appropriate tool in the toolbox?

Ensure Fiscal Sustainability

Our previous work has shown that transportation funding, and the Highway Trust Fund in particular, faces an imbalance of revenues and expenditures and other threats to its long term sustainability. Furthermore, the sustainability of transportation funding should also be seen in the context of the broader, governmentwide problem of fiscal imbalance. The federal role in transportation funding must be reexamined to ensure that it is sustainable in this new fiscal reality. A sustainable surface transportation program will require targeted investment, with adequate return on investment, from not only the federal government but also state and local governments and the private sector.

The following illustrative questions can be used to determine the extent to which proposals to restructure and fund surface transportation programs ensure fiscal sustainability.

- To what extent do the proposals reexamine current and future spending on surface transportation programs?
- Are the recommendations affordable and financially stable over the long-term? To what extent are the recommendations placed in the context of federal deficits, constrained budgets, and other spending commitments, and to what extent do they meet a rigorous examination of the use of federal funds?
- To what extent are recommendations considered in the context of trends that could affect the transportation system in the future, such as population growth, increased fuel efficiency, and increased freight traffic?

Current concerns about the sustainability and performance of existing programs suggest that this is an opportune time for Congress to more clearly define the federal role in transportation and improve progress toward specific, nationally defined outcomes. Given the scope of the needed transformation, it may be necessary to shift policies and programs incrementally or on a pilot basis to gain practical lessons for a coherent, sustainable, and effective national program and funding structure to best serve the nation for the 21st century.

Various Options Are Available or Have Been Proposed to Fund Investments in the Nation's Infrastructure

Absent changes in planned spending, a variety of funding and financing options will likely be needed to address projected transportation funding shortfalls. Although some of the demand for additional investment in transportation could be reduced, there is a growing consensus that some level of additional investment in transportation is warranted. A range of options—from altering existing or introducing new funding approaches to employing various financing mechanisms—could be used to help meet the demand for additional investments. Each of these options has different merits and challenges, and the selection of any of them will likely involve trade-offs among different policy goals. Furthermore, the suitability of any of these options depends on the level of federal involvement or control that policymakers desire for a given area of policy. However, as we have reported, when infrastructure investment decisions are made based on sound evaluations, these options can lead to an appropriate blend of public and private funds to match public and private costs and benefits.[10]

Existing Strategies Can Help Reduce the Demand for Additional Investment

Estimates from multiple sources indicate that additional investment in the transportation system could be warranted. For example, in its January 2008 report, the National Surface Transportation Policy and Revenue Study Commission (Policy Commission) recommended an annual investment of about $225 billion from all levels of government in the surface transportation system—an increase of about $140 billion from current spending levels.[11] Similarly, the Congressional Budget Office recently estimated that an annual investment of about $165 billion in surface transportation could be economically justifiable.[12] In addition, in its February 2008 interim report, the National Surface Transportation Infrastructure Financing Commission (Financing Commission) noted that one of its base assumptions is that there is a gap between current funding levels and investment needs.[13]

However, some of the demand for additional investment in transportation infrastructure could be reduced. We have previously reported that the ways in which revenue is generated and distributed can influence the decisions made by users as well as decision-making and programs at the state and local levels.[14] In particular, our previous work has shown that current funding and decision-making processes provide a built-in preference for projects that build or maintain transportation infrastructure rather than try to use existing infrastructure more efficiently—which would reduce the overall demand for additional investments. CBO also recently reported that some of the demand for additional spending on infrastructure could be met by providing incentives to use existing infrastructure more efficiently. In its February 2008 interim report, the Financing Commission noted the need to use new approaches and technologies to maximize the use of current capacity.

We have also previously reported that increased federal highway grants influence states and localities to substitute federal funds for funds they otherwise would have spent on highways for other purposes.

Consequently, additional federal investments in transportation do not necessarily translate into commensurate levels of spending by the states and localities on transportation. Addressing this "leakage" with such tools as maintenance-of-effort requirements could maximize the effectiveness of federal investments.

The principles we have identified for restructuring the surface transportation programs can also be used as a framework for considering levels of investment and the funding and financing options described below. For example, in defining the federal role in funding transportation, we have previously reported that where the national interest is greatest, having the federal government fund a higher share of program costs could be appropriate. Conversely, where the national interest is less evident, state and local governments, and others could assume more responsibility. In addition, incorporating incentives or penalty provisions into different funding and financing approaches can help ensure performance and accountability.

Funding Approaches Can Be Altered or Developed to Help Fund Infrastructure Investments

Various existing funding approaches could be altered or new funding approaches could be developed, to help fund investments in the nation's infrastructure. These various approaches can be grouped into two categories: taxes and user fees.

A variety of taxes have been and could be used to fund the nation's infrastructure, including excise, sales, property, and income taxes. For example, federal excise taxes on motor fuels are the primary source of funding for the federal surface transportation program. Fuel taxes are attractive because they have provided a relatively stable stream of revenues and the collection and enforcement costs are relatively low. However, fuel taxes do not currently convey to drivers the full costs of their use of the road—such as the costs of wear and tear, congestion, and pollution. Moreover, federal motor fuel taxes have not been increased since 1993—and thus the purchasing power of fuel tax revenues has eroded with inflation. As CBO has previously reported, the existing fuel taxes could be altered in a variety of ways to address this erosion, including increasing the per-gallon tax rate and indexing the rates to inflation.[15] Some transportation stakeholders have suggested exploring the potential of using a carbon tax, or other carbon pricing strategies, to help fund infrastructure investments.[16] In a system of carbon taxes, fossil fuel emissions would be taxed, with the tax proportional to the amount of carbon dioxide released in its combustion. Because a carbon tax could have a broad effect on consumer decisions, we have previously reported that it could be used to complement Corporate Average Fuel Economy standards, which require manufacturers meet fuel economy standards for passenger cars and light trucks to reduce oil consumption.[17] A carbon tax would create incentives that could affect a broader range of consumer choices as well as provide revenue for infrastructure.

Another funding source for infrastructure is user fees. The concept underlying user fees—that is, users pay directly for the infrastructure they use—is a long-standing aspect of many infrastructure programs. Examples of user fees that could be altered or introduced include fees based on vehicle miles traveled (VMT) on roadways; freight fees, such as a per-container charge; congestion pricing of roads; and tolling.

- **VMT Fees.** To more directly reflect the amount a vehicle uses the road, users could be charged a fee based on the number of vehicle miles traveled. In 2006, the Oregon Department of Transportation conducted a pilot program designed to test the technological and administrative feasibility of a VMT fee. The pilot program demonstrated that a VMT fee could be implemented to replace the fuel tax as the principal source of transportation revenue by utilizing a Global Positioning System (GPS) to track miles driven and collecting the VMT fee ($0.012 per mile traveled) at fuel pumps that can read information from the GPS.[18] As we have previously reported, using a GPS could also track mileage in high congestion zones, and the fee could be adjusted upward for miles driven in these areas or during more congested times of day such as rush hour—a strategy that might reduce congestion and save fuel.[19] In addition, the system could be designed to apply different fees to vehicles, depending on their fuel economy. On the federal level, a VMT fee could be based on odometer readings, which would likely be a simpler and less costly way to implement such a program. A VMT fee—unless it is adjusted based on the fuel economy of the vehicle—does not provide incentives for customers to buy vehicles with higher fuel economy ratings because the fee depends only on mileage. Also, because the fee would likely be collected from individual drivers, a VMT fee could be expensive for the government to implement, potentially making it a less cost-effective approach than a motor fuel or carbon tax. The Oregon study also identified other challenges including concerns about privacy and technical difficulties in retrofitting vehicles with the necessary technology.

- **Freight Fees.** Given the importance of freight movement to the economy, the Policy Commission recently recommended a new federal freight fee to support the development of a national program aimed at strategically expanding capacity for freight transportation.[20] While the volume of domestic and international freight moving through the country has increased dramatically and is expected to continue growing, the capacity of the nation's freight transportation infrastructure has not increased at the same rate as demand.[21] To support the development of a national program for freight transportation, the Policy Commission recommended the introduction of a federal freight fee. The Policy Commission notes that a freight fee, such as a per-container charge, could help fund projects that remedy chokepoints and increase throughput. The Policy Commission also recommended that a portion of the customs duties, which are assessed on imported goods, be used to fund capacity improvements for freight transportation. The majority of customs duties currently collected, however, are deposited in the U.S. Treasury's general fund for the general support of federal activities.[22] Therefore, designating a portion of customs duties for surface transportation funding would not create a new source of revenue, but rather transfer funds from the general fund.

- **Congestion Pricing.** As we have previously reported, congestion pricing, or road pricing, attempts to influence driver behavior by charging fees during peak hours to encourage users to shift to off-peak periods, use less congested routes, or use alternative modes. Congestion pricing can also help guide capital investment decisions for new transportation infrastructure. In particular, as congestion increases, toll rates also increase, and such increases (sometimes referred to as "congestion surcharges") signal increased demand for physical capacity, indicating where capital investments to increase capacity would be most valuable. Furthermore, these congestion surcharges can potentially enhance mobility by reducing congestion and the demand for roads when the surcharges vary according to congestion to maintain a predetermined level of service. The most common form of congestion pricing in the United States is high-occupancy toll lanes, which are priced lanes that offer drivers of vehicles that do not meet the occupancy requirements the option of paying a toll to use lanes that are otherwise restricted for high-occupancy vehicles.

Various Financing Mechanisms Can Also Help Fund Infrastructure Projects

Financing mechanisms can provide flexibility for all levels of government when funding additional infrastructure projects, particularly when traditional pay-as-you-go funding approaches, such as taxes or fees, are not set at high enough levels to meet demands. The federal government currently offers several programs to provide state and local governments with incentives such as bonds, loans, and credit assistance to help finance infrastructure. Financing mechanisms can create potential savings by accelerating projects to offset rapidly increasing construction costs and offer incentives for investment from state and local governments and from the private sector. However, each financing strategy is, in the final analysis, a form of debt that ultimately must be repaid with interest. Furthermore, since the federal government's cost of capital is lower than that of the private sector, financing mechanisms, such as bonding, may be more expensive than timely, full, and up-front appropriations. Finally, if the federal government chooses to finance infrastructure projects, policy makers must decide how borrowed dollars will be repaid, either by users or by the general population either now or in the future through increases in taxes or reductions in other government services.

A number of available mechanisms can be used to help finance infrastructure projects. Examples of these financing mechanisms follow.

- **Bonding.** A number of bonding strategies—including tax-exempt bonds,[23] private activity bonds, Grant Anticipation Revenue Vehicles (GARVEE) bonds, and Grant Anticipation Notes (GAN)—offer flexibility to bridge funding gaps when traditional revenue sources are scarce. For example, state-issued GARVEE or GAN bonds provide capital in advance of expected federal funds, allowing states to accelerate highway and transit project construction and thus potentially reduce construction costs. Through April 2008, 20 states and two territories issued approximately $8.2 billion of GARVEE-type debt financing and 20 other states are actively considering bonding or seeking legislative authority to issue GARVEEs. Furthermore, SAFETEA-LU authorized the Secretary of

Transportation to allocate $15 billion in tax-exempt bonds for qualified highway and surface freight transfer facilities. To date, $5.3 billion has been allocated for six projects. Several bills have been introduced in this Congress that would increase investment in the nation's infrastructure through bonding. For example, the Build America Bonds Act would provide $50 billion in new infrastructure funding through bonding. Although bonds can provide up-front capital for infrastructure projects, they can be more expensive for the federal government than traditional federal grants. This higher expense results, in part, because the government must compensate the investors for the risks they assume through an adequate return on their investment.

- **Loans, Loan Guarantees, and Credit Assistance.** The federal government currently has two programs designed to offer credit assistance for surface transportation projects. The Transportation Infrastructure Finance and Innovation Act of 1998 (TIFIA) authorized the Federal Highway Administration to provide credit assistance, in the form of direct loans, loan guarantees, and standby lines of credit for projects of national significance. A similar program, Railroad Rehabilitation and Improvement Financing (RRIF), offers loans to acquire, improve, develop, or rehabilitate intermodal or rail equipment and develop new intermodal railroad facilities. To date, 15 TIFIA projects have been approved totaling over $4.8 billion in credit assistance and the RRIF program has approved 21 loan agreements worth more than $747 million. These programs are designed to leverage federal funds by attracting substantial nonfederal investments in infrastructure projects. However, the federal government assumes a level of risk when it makes or guarantees loans for projects financed with private investment.[24]

- **Revolving funds.** Revolving funds can be used to dedicate capital to be loaned for qualified infrastructure projects. In general, loaned dollars are repaid, recycled back into the revolving fund, and subsequently reinvested in the infrastructure through additional loans. Such funds exist at both the federal and the state levels and are used to finance various infrastructure projects ranging from highways to water mains. For example, two federal funds support water infrastructure financing, the Clean Water State Revolving Fund for wastewater facilities, and the Drinking Water State Revolving Fund for drinking water facilities. Under each of these programs, the federal government provides seed money to states, which they supplement with their own funds. These funds are then loaned to local governments and other entities for water infrastructure construction and upgrades and various water quality projects. In addition, State Infrastructure Banks (SIBs)—capitalized with federal and state matching funds—are state-run revolving funds that make loans and provide credit enhancements and other forms of nongrant assistance to infrastructure projects. Through June 2007, 33 SIBs have made approximately 596 loan agreements worth about $6.2 billion to leverage other available funds for transportation projects across the nation.[25] Furthermore, other funds—such as a dedicated national infrastructure bank—have been proposed to increase investment in infrastructure with a national or regional significance. A challenge for revolving funds in general is maintaining their capitalized value. Defaults on loans and inflation can reduce the capitalized value of the fund—necessitating an infusion of capital needed to continue the fund's operations.

Highway Public-Private Partnerships Hold Promise, but Also Raise a Number of Issues to Consider

Another important and emerging vehicle for funding investments in transportation is public-private partnerships. In February 2008 we reported on highway public-private partnerships. These arrangements show promise as a viable alternative, where appropriate, to help meet growing and costly transportation demands and have the potential to provide numerous benefits to the public sector.[26] The highway public-private partnerships created to date have resulted in advantages from the perspective of state and local governments, such as the construction of new infrastructure without using public funding, and obtaining funds by extracting value from existing facilities for reinvestment in transportation and other public programs. For example, the state of Indiana received $3.8 billion from leasing the Indiana Toll Road and used those proceeds to fund a 10-year statewide transportation plan. Highway public-private partnerships potentially provide other benefits, including the transfer or sharing of project risks to the private sector. Such risks include those associated with construction costs and schedules and having sufficient levels of traffic and revenues to be financially viable. In addition, the public sector can potentially benefit from increased efficiencies in operations and life-cycle management, such as increased use of innovative technologies. Finally, through the use of tolling, highway public-private partnerships offer the potential to price highways to better reflect the true costs of operating and maintaining them and to increase mobility by adjusting tolls to manage demand, as well as the potential for more cost effective investment decisions by private investors.

Highway public-private partnerships also entail potential costs and risks. Most importantly, there is no "free" money in public-private partnerships. While highway public-private partnerships can be used to obtain financing for highways, these funds are largely a new source of borrowed funds—a form of privately issued debt that must be repaid to private investors seeking a return on their investment by road users over what potentially could be a period of several generations. Though concession agreements can limit the extent to which a concessionaire can raise tolls, it is likely that tolls will increase on a privately operated highway to a greater extent than they would on a publicly operated toll road. To the extent that a private concessionaire gains market power by control of a road where there are not other viable travel alternatives, the potential also exists that the public could pay tolls that are higher than tolls based on the cost of the facilities, including a reasonable rate of return. Additionally, because large up-front concession payments have, in part, been used to fund immediate needs, it remains to be seen whether these agreements will provide long-term benefits to future generations who will potentially be paying progressively higher toll rates throughout the length of a concession agreement. Highway public-private partnerships are also potentially more costly than traditional public procurement—for example, there are costs associated with the need to hire financial and legal advisors.

In short, while highway public-private partnerships have promise, they are not a panacea for meeting all transportation system demands. Ultimately the extent to which public-private partnerships can be used as a tool to help meet the nation's transportation financing challenges will depend on the ability of states to effectively manage and implement them. For example, states must have appropriate enabling legislation in place and the institutional ability to manage complex contractual mechanisms—either in the form of in-house expertise or through contractors. Most importantly, the extent to which public-private partnerships can be used as a tool to help meet the nation's transportation funding challenges will depend on how well states are able to weigh public interest considerations. The benefits of public-private partnerships are potential benefits—that is, they are not assured and can only be achieved by weighing them against potential costs and trade-offs through careful, comprehensive analysis to determine whether public-private partnerships are appropriate in specific circumstances and, if so, how best to implement them, and how best to protect the public interest.

In considering the numerous issues surrounding the protection of the public interest, we reached the following conclusions in our February 2008 report on highway public-private partnerships:

- First, consideration of highway public-private partnerships could benefit from more consistent, rigorous, systematic, and up-front analysis. While highway public-private partnerships are fairly new in the United States, and although they are meant to serve the public interest, it is difficult to be confident that these interests are being protected when formal identification and consideration of public and national interests has been lacking, and where limited up-front analysis of public interest issues using established criteria has been conducted. Partnerships to date have identified and protected the public interest largely through terms contained in concession contracts, including maintenance and expansion requirements, protections for the workforce, and oversight and monitoring mechanisms to ensure that private partners fulfilled their obligations. While these protections are important, governments in other countries, including Australia and the United Kingdom, have developed systematic approaches to identifying and evaluating public interest before agreements are entered into, including the use of public interest criteria, as well as assessment tools, and require their use when considering private investments in public infrastructure. For example, a state government in Australia uses a public interest test to determine how the public interest would be affected in eight specific areas, including whether the views and rights of affected communities have been heard and protected and whether the process is sufficiently transparent. While similar tools have been used to some extent in the United States, their use has been more limited. Using up-front public interest analysis tools can also assist public agencies in determining the expected benefits and costs of a project and an appropriate means to deliver the project. Not using such tools may lead to certain aspects of protecting public interest being overlooked.

- Second, fresh thinking is needed on the appropriate federal approach. DOT has done much to promote the benefits, but comparatively little to either assist states and localities in weighing potential costs and trade-offs, nor to assess how potentially important national interests might be protected in highway public-private partnerships. This is in many respects a function of the design of the federal program as few mechanisms exist to identify potential national interests in cases where federal funds have not or will not be used. For example, although the Indiana Toll Road is part of the Interstate Highway System and most traffic on the road is interstate in nature, federal officials had little involvement in reviewing the terms of this concession agreement because minimal federal funds were used to construct it, and those funds were repaid to the federal government. The historic test of the presence of federal funding may have been relevant at a time when the federal government played a larger role in financing highways but may no longer be relevant when there are new players and multiple sources of financing, including potentially significant private money. Reexamining the federal role in transportation provides an opportunity to identify the emerging national public interests in highway public-private partnerships and determine how highway public-private partnerships fit in with national programs.

On the basis of these conclusions, we recommended that Congress direct the Secretary of Transportation to develop and submit objective criteria for identifying national public interests in highway public-private partnerships, including any additional legal authority, guidance, or assessment tools that would be appropriately required.[27] We are pleased to note that in a recent testimony before the House, the Secretary indicated a willingness to begin developing such criteria. This is no easy task, however. The recent Policy Commission report illustrates the challenges of identifying national public interests as the Policy Commission's recommendations for future restrictions—including limiting allowable toll increases and requiring concessionaires to share revenues with the public sector—stood in sharp contrast to the dissenting views of three commissioners. We believe any potential federal restrictions on highway public-private partnerships must be carefully crafted to avoid undermining the potential benefits that can be achieved. Reexamining the federal role in transportation provides an opportunity for DOT we believe, to play a targeted role in ensuring that national interests are considered, as appropriate.

CONCLUDING OBSERVATIONS

The nation's surface transportation programs are no longer producing the desired results. The reliability of the nation's surface transportation system is declining as congestion continues to grow. Although infusing surface transportation programs with additional funding, especially in light of the projected shortfalls in the Highway Trust Fund, could be viewed as a quick and direct solution, past experience shows that increased funding for the program does not necessarily translate into improved performance. Furthermore, the nation's current fiscal outlook may make such solutions fiscally imprudent. In addition, before additional federal funds are committed to the nation's surface transportation programs, we believe a fundamental reexamination of the program is warranted. Such a reexamination would require reviewing the results of surface transportation programs and testing their continued relevance and relative priority. Appropriate funding sources and financing mechanisms can then be tailored for programs that continue to be relevant in today's environment and address a national interest, such as freight movement.

Over the coming months, various options to restructure and fund surface transportation programs will likely be put forward by a range of transportation stakeholders. Ultimately, Congress and other federal policymakers will have to determine which option—or which combination of options—best meets the nation's needs. There is no silver bullet that can solve the nation's transportation challenges, and many of the options, such as allowing greater private-sector investment in the nation's infrastructure, could be politically difficult to implement both nationally and locally. The principles that we identified provide a framework for evaluating these various options. Although the principles do not prescribe a specific approach to restructuring and funding the programs, they do provide key attributes that will help ensure that a restructured surface transportation program addresses current challenges. We will continue to assist the Congress as it works to evaluate the various options and develop a national transportation policy for the 21st century that improves the design of transportation programs, the delivery of services, and accountability for results.

Mr. Chairman, this concludes my prepared statement. I would be pleased to respond to any questions that you or other Members of the Committee might have.

Related GAO Products

Federal User Fees: A Design Guide, GAO-08-386SP. Washington, D.C.: May 29, 2008.

Physical Infrastructure: Challenges and Investment Options for the Nation's Infrastructure, GAO-08-763T. Washington, D.C.: May 8, 2008.

Surface Transportation: Restructured Federal Approach Needed for More Focused, Performance-Based, and Sustainable Programs, GAO-08-400. Washington, D.C.: March 6, 2008.

Highway Public-Private Partnerships: More Rigorous Up-front Analysis Could Better Secure Potential Benefits and Protect the Public Interest, GAO-08-44. Washington, D.C.: February 8, 2008.

Surface Transportation: Preliminary Observations on Efforts to Restructure Current Program, GAO-08-478T. Washington, D.C.: February 6, 2008.

Congressional Directives: Selected Agencies' Processes for Responding to Funding Instructions, GAO-08-209. Washington, D.C.: January 31, 2008.

Long-Term Fiscal Outlook: Action Is Needed to Avoid the Possibility of a Serious Economic Disruption in the Future, GAO-08-411T. Washington, D.C.: January 29, 2008.

Federal-Aid Highways: Increased Reliance on Contractors Can Pose Oversight Challenges for Federal and State Officials, GAO-08-198. Washington, D.C.: January 8, 2008.

Freight Transportation: National Policy and Strategies Can Help Improve Freight Mobility. GAO-08-287. Washington, D.C.: January 7, 2008.

A Call For Stewardship: Enhancing the Federal Government's Ability to Address Key Fiscal and Other 21st Century Challenges. GAO-08-93SP. Washington, D.C.: December 17, 2007.

Transforming Transportation Policy for the 21st Century: Highlights of a Forum. GAO-07-1210SP. Washington, D.C.: September 19, 2007.

Surface Transportation: Strategies Are Available for Making Existing Road Infrastructure Perform Better. GAO-07-920. Washington, D.C.: July 26, 2007.

Intermodal Transportation: DOT Could Take Further Actions to Address Intermodal Barriers. GAO-07-718. Washington, D.C.: June 20, 2007.

Performance and Accountability: Transportation Challenges Facing Congress and the Department of Transportation. GAO-07-545T. Washington, D.C.: March 6, 2007.

High-Risk Series: An Update. GAO-07-310. Washington, D.C.: January 2007.

Highway Finance: States' Expanding Use of Tolling Illustrates Diverse Challenges and Strategies. GAO-06-554. Washington, D.C.: June 28, 2006.

Highway Congestion: Intelligent Transportation Systems' Promise for Managing Congestion Falls Short, and DOT Could Better Facilitate Their Strategic Use. GAO-05-943. Washington, D.C.: September 14, 2005.

21st Century Challenges: Reexamining the Base of the Federal Government. GAO-05-325SP. Washington, D.C.: February 1, 2005.

Highway and Transit Investments: Options for Improving Information on Projects' Benefits and Costs and Increasing Accountability for Results. GAO-05-172. Washington, D.C.: January 24, 2005.

Federal-Aid Highways: Trends, Effect on State Spending, and Options for Future Program Design. GAO-04-802. Washington, D.C.: August 31, 2004.

Marine Transportation: Federal Financing and a Framework for Infrastructure Investments. GAO-02-1033. Washington, D.C.: September 9, 2002.

End Notes

[1] GAO's audits and evaluations identify federal programs and operations that, in some cases, are high risk because of their greater vulnerabilities to fraud, waste, abuse, and mismanagement. In recent years, we also have identified high-risk areas to focus on the need for broad-based transformations to address major economy, efficiency, or effectiveness challenges. Since 1990, we have periodically reported on government operations that we have designated as high risk. In 2007, we added financing the nation's transportation system to the High Risk List. See, GAO, *High-Risk Series: An Update*. GAO-07-310 (Washington, D.C.: January 2007).

[2] GAO, *Long-Term Fiscal Outlook: Action Is Needed to Avoid the Possibility of a Serious Economic Disruption in the Future*, GAO-08-411T (Washington, D.C.: Jan. 29, 2008) and *Fiscal Stewardship: A Critical Challenge Facing Our Nation*, GAO-07-362SP (Washington, D.C.: January 2007).

[3] See GAO, *Performance and Accountability: Transportation Challenges Facing Congress and the Department of Transportation*, GAO-07-545T (Washington, D.C.: Mar. 6, 2007) and *21st Century Challenges: Reexamining the Base of the Federal Government,* GAO-05-325SP (Washington, D.C.: February 2005).

[4] See "Related GAO Products" at the end of this testimony statement. These previous performance audits were conducted in accordance with generally accepted government auditing standards.

[5] GAO, *Highway Public-Private Partnerships: More Rigorous Up-front Analysis Could Better Secure Potential Benefits and Protect the Public Interest,* GAO-08-44 (Washington, D.C.: Feb. 8, 2008).

[6] GAO, *Highway and Transit Investments: Options for Improving Information on Projects' Benefits and Costs and Increasing Accountability for Results,* GAO-05-172 (Washington, D.C.: Jan. 24, 2005).

[7] CBO, *Status of the Highway Trust Fund*: 2007 (Washington, D.C.: Mar. 27, 2007).

[8] GAO, *Surface Transportation: Restructured Federal Approach Needed for More Focused, Performance-Based, and Sustainable Programs*, GAO-08-400 (Washington, D.C.: Mar. 6, 2008).

[9] GAO, *Freight Transportation: National Policy and Strategies Can Help Improve Freight Mobility.* GAO-08-287 (Washington, D.C.: Jan. 7, 2008).

[10] GAO, *Freight Transportation: Strategies Needed to Address Planning and Financing Limitations,* GAO-04-165 (Washington D.C.: Dec. 19, 2003).

[11] Congress established the Policy Commission in SAFETEA-LU. The mission of the Policy Commission was, among other things, to examine the condition and future needs of the nation's surface transportation system and short and long-term alternatives to replace or supplement the fuel tax as the principal revenue source to support the Highway Trust Fund. In January 2008, the Policy Commission released its final report with numerous recommendations to reform the current structure of the nation's surface transportation programs.

[12] CBO, *Current and Future Investment in Infrastructure*, (Washington, D.C.: May 8, 2008). CBO defines economic justifiable investments as investments whose private and social benefits would be at least equal to their economic costs.

[13] Congress created the Financing Commission in SAFETEA-LU and charged it with analyzing future highway and transit needs and the finances of the Highway Trust Fund and recommending alternative approaches to financing transportation infrastructure.

[14] GAO, *Surface Transportation: Strategies Are Available for Making Existing Road Infrastructure Perform Better,* GAO-07-920 (Washington, D.C.: July 26, 2007).

[15] CBO, *Status of the Highway Trust Fund: 2007* (Washington, D.C.: Mar. 27, 2007).

[16] Another carbon pricing strategy is a cap-and-trade program, which combines a regulatory limit or cap on the amount of carbon that can be emitted into the atmosphere with market elements such as the opportunity to buy additional allowances to emit additional carbon. Auctioning the allowances of a cap-and-trade program would generate revenue for the government, which could be used for a variety of purposes, including infrastructure investments.

[17] GAO, *Vehicle Fuel Economy: Reforming Fuel Economy Standards Could Help Reduce Oil Consumption by Cars and Light Trucks, and Other Options Could Complement These Standards*, GAO-07-921 (Washington, D.C.: Aug. 2, 2007).

[18] Oregon's Mileage Fee Concept and Road User Fee Pilot Program: Final Report.

[19] GAO-07-921.

[20] *Transportation for Tomorrow: Report of the National Surface Transportation Policy and Revenue Study* Commission, January 2008.

[21] GAO, *Freight Transportation: National Policy and Strategies Can Help Improve Freight Mobility*, GAO-08-287 (Washington, D.C.: Jan. 7, 2008).

[22] GAO, *Marine Transportation: Federal Financing and a Framework for Infrastructure Investments*, GAO-02-1033 (Washington, D.C.: Sept. 9, 2002).

[23] Tax-exempt bonds are government bonds that are used for purposes such as infrastructure, schools, libraries, general municipal expenditures, or refunding of old debt. Tax-exempt means that the interest paid to bondholders is generally not included in their gross income for federal income tax purposes. Examples of tax-exempt bonds include municipal bonds and private activity bonds that allow tax-exempt debt to be used by private entities to help finance qualified facilities.

[24] According to DOT, federal requirements necessitate that a credit risk premium be provided to insure the federal government against the risk of loans defaulting. As a result, these loans are closely examined for risk of loss and, to date, none of the TIFIA or RRIF loans have defaulted.

[25] Eight states—Arizona, Florida, Minnesota, Missouri, Ohio, South Carolina, Texas, and Wyoming—account for 95 percent of the total loan agreements reached through fiscal year 2006.

[26] See GAO-08-44. We focused our review on highway public-private partnerships in which the public sector enters into a lease or concession agreement with the private sector to provide transportation services for an extended period of time, and where the private sector receives some or all toll revenues over the life of the agreement. We recognize that the term public-private partnerships can be applied to other types of highway projects and other types of transportation projects (such as mass transit and freight rail projects), as well as projects outside the transportation sector (such as hospitals and prisons). We did not include any of these in the scope of our review and my testimony today cannot necessarily be extrapolated to these or other types of public-private partnerships.

[27] To ensure that future highway public-private partnerships meet federal requirements concerning the use of excess revenues for federally eligible transportation purposes, we also recommended that the Secretary of Transportation direct the Federal Highway Administrator to clarify federal-aid highway regulations on the methodology for determining excess toll revenue, including the reasonable rate of return to private investors in highway public-private partnerships that involve federal investment.

In: Surface Transportation: Infrastructure, … ISBN: 978-1-60692-357-3
Editor: Keith A. Libermann, PP: 113-134© 2010 Nova Science Publishers, Inc.

Chapter 3

PUBLIC SPENDING ON SURFACE TRANSPORTATION INFRASTRUCTURE

Congressional Budget Office

Chairman Spratt, Congressman Ryan, and Members of the Committee, thank you for the invitation to discuss public spending on surface transportation infrastructure. The Congressional Budget Office (CBO) projects that the balance in the Highway Trust Fund will be exhausted at some point during fiscal year 2009. In addition, the Safe, Accountable, Flexible, Efficient Transportation Equity Act: A Legacy for Users (SAFETEA-LU) expires at the end of that fiscal year. Consequently, the Congress will face important policy questions about how much to invest in surface transportation systems; how to apportion that spending among roads, rail, transit, and other modes of transportation; how best to finance that spending; and which levels of government are best positioned to make those decisions.

To shed light on those issues, my statement today describes recent trends in public spending for infrastructure at all levels, the role of Highway Trust Fund in accounting for such spending, and some options for financing future spending on transportation infrastructure.

In my testimony, I will make the following points:

- Spending on surface transportation infrastructure by all levels of government in 2004 was $191 billion (in 2006 dollars), or 1.5 percent of gross domestic product (GDP). The federal government provided about one-quarter of those funds, and states and localities provided the rest. Those funds were split about equally between spending for capital projects and operation and maintenance. Most of that spending was for roads.

- Federal outlays are directed almost entirely to capital projects and account for slightly less than one-half of all public spending on such projects. In contrast, state and local governments provide virtually all of the public spending to operate and maintain the surface transportation infrastructure.
- Most of the federal spending for infrastructure comes from excise taxes on gasoline and diesel fuel and other taxes that are credited to the Highway Trust Fund. In recent years, spending from the highway account of the trust fund has consistently exceeded its income. According to CBO's projections, if annual spending continues at its currently authorized levels (adjusted for inflation after 2009), the highway account of the trust fund will be exhausted at some point during fiscal year 2009; the mass transit account will have sufficient revenues to cover its expenditures until 2012.
- Over the 2009–2017 period, policymakers face a growing differential between expected revenues in the highway account and spending from that account that could occur if obligations continue at the levels authorized in SAFETEA-LU, adjusted for inflation. Eliminating that differential would require a cut in spending authority of 40 percent below projected levels during 2009 and about 20 percent annually thereafter through 2017; an increase in revenues of about 20 percent over the period; or some combination of the two approaches.
- The current system of generating revenues to fund surface transportation projects relies primarily on various excise taxes. Under current law, those taxes are not sufficient to pay for rising highway construction costs or to account for the external costs of pollution or congestion. To balance the trust fund's spending and revenues, tax rates could be increased or indexed. However, because the taxes are not linked to the use of specific roads, they do not provide signals to policymakers indicating which are most valuable to users.
- As an alternative to the current system, existing taxes could be replaced or supplemented with charges to users based on the costs that they impose on the system and the external costs of pollution and congestion. For example, tolls or fees based on mileage or vehicle weight may provide users a clearer signal of the costs that they

impose on the system. Even so, such user charges by themselves may not be able to finance the entire highway system, and their administrative feasibility over a nationwide system of roads has not yet been demonstrated.

TRENDS IN PUBLIC SPENDING ON SURFACE TRANSPORTATION INFRASTRUCTURE

The federal government and state and local governments devote substantial resources to building, operating, and maintaining the nation's surface transportation infrastructure. During 2004, which is the most recent year for which comprehensive data are available, total public spending on surface transportation infrastructure was $191 billion (measured in 2006 dollars), or 1.5 percent of GDP. Those figures include spending by federal, state, and local governments on roads, rail, mass transit, and water transportation. Since 1956, annual public spending on such infrastructure has ranged between 1.4 percent and 2.0 percent of GDP.[1]

In 2004, about half of total public spending on surface transportation infrastructure went to capital projects, for example, building or rehabilitating physical infrastructure. The other half was spent on operating and maintaining that infrastructure. The shares of capital expenditures and operation and maintenance expenditures within the total have been fairly stable since the mid-1980s. Before then, capital expenditures usually exceeded spending on operation and maintenance (see Figure 1). Measured in 2006 dollars, spending for operation and maintenance has trended steadily upward over the past 50 years. Measured the same way, capital spending for surface transportation peaked in the late 1960s (in part because of the construction of the Interstate Highway System), declined through the early 1 980s, and has grown steadily since then.

Spending priorities on surface transportation infrastructure vary by level of government. In 2004, federal outlays—almost entirely in the form of grants and loans to states and localities—principally funded capital projects; 92 cents of every federal dollar spent on such infrastructure was for capital projects rather than operation and maintenance. In contrast, the majority of state and local spending (64 percent) was allocated to operation and maintenance. The federal government provided almost one-half (46 percent) of total public funding for surface transportation capital projects, and states and localities accounted for virtually all (96 percent) of public spending to operate and maintain that infrastructure.[2]

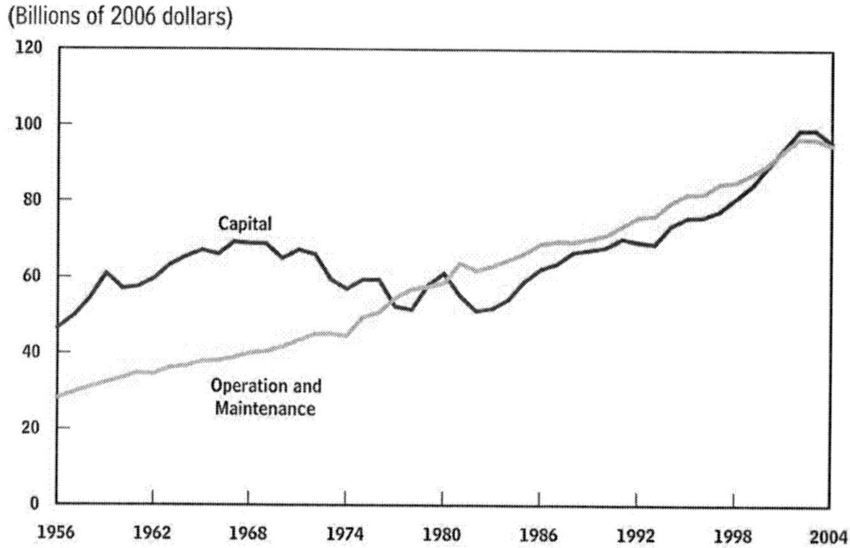

Figure 1. Federal, State, and Local Spending for Surface Transportation Capital Investments and Operation and Maintenance, 1956 to 2004.

Among types of surface transportation, roads account for the largest share of infrastructure spending by any level of government (see Figure 2). About 80 percent of capital spending on surface transportation infrastructure by the federal government and state and local governments (net of federal grants and loan subsidies) goes to roads. Roads also account for a large portion of spending to operate and maintain surface transportation infrastructure, though that share is considerably larger at the state and local levels than at the federal level (64 percent versus 30 percent, respectively).

Federal spending on surface transportation infrastructure in 2007 was about $50 billion.[3] The federal government supplied about one-quarter of all public funding for surface transportation infrastructure, with state and local governments providing the rest. That share has been roughly stable over the past several decades.

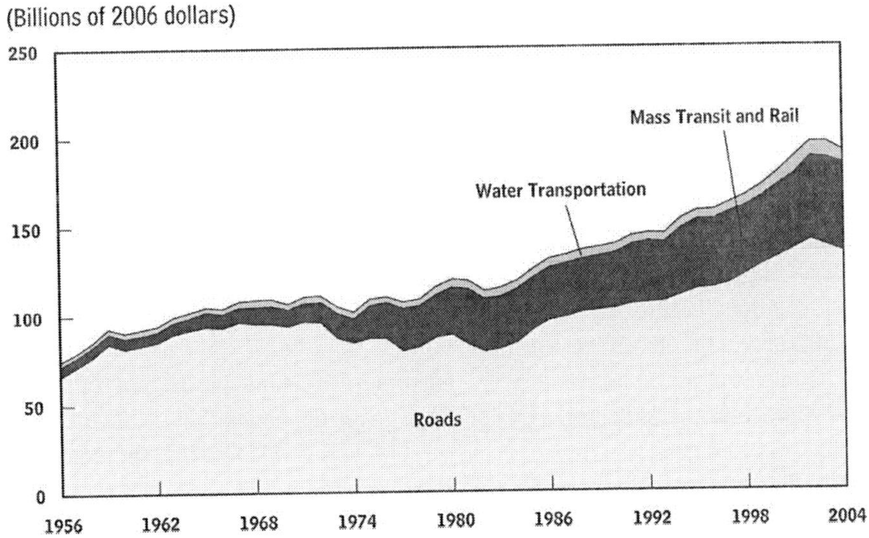

Figure 2. Federal, State, and Local Spending on Surface Transportation Infrastructure, by Type, 1956 to 2004.

In addition to government, private entities play a limited role in providing surface transportation infrastructure beyond simply supplying services under contract to a government agency. Such participation by the private sector, which is often referred to as public–private partnerships, has so far constituted only a relatively small amount of infrastructure funding. Under the Transportation Infrastructure Finance and Innovation Act (TIFIA) of 1998 (Public Law 105-178), the federal government has encouraged private investment to improve the nation's surface transportation system by providing direct loans at below-market rates and loan guarantees—at a cost of $240 million through 2006.

OVERVIEW OF THE HIGHWAY TRUST FUND

The federal government's surface transportation programs are financed mostly through the Highway Trust Fund (certain transit programs receive appropriations from the U.S. Treasury's general fund). Those surface transportation programs are administered by the Federal Highway Administration (FHWA) and the Federal Transit Administration.[4]

The Highway Trust Fund is an accounting mechanism in the federal budget. The fund comprises two separate accounts, one for highways and one for mass transit. It records specific cash inflows (revenues from certain excise taxes on motor fuels and trucks) and cash outflows (spending on designated highway and mass transit programs). By far, the largest component of the trust fund is the Federal-Aid Highway program (see Table 1).

Spending from the Highway Trust Fund is not automatically triggered by tax revenues credited to it. Authorization acts provide budget authority for highway programs, mostly in the form of contract authority (the authority to incur obligations in advance of appropriations). Annual spending from the fund is largely controlled by limits on the amount of contract authority that can be obligated in a particular year.

Such obligation limitations are customarily set in annual appropriation acts. The most recent authorization law governing spending from the trust fund— SAFETEA-LU—was enacted in 2005 and is due to expire at the end of 2009. The law provides specific amounts of contract authority over the 2005–2009 period and authorizes appropriations for certain programs that are not funded through contract authority. It also specifies annual obligation limitations, which may be superseded each year by limitations set in appropriation acts.

The largest source of revenues credited to the Highway Trust Fund is the tax of 18.3 cents per gallon on gasoline and gasohol. Under current law, such taxes are scheduled to expire in 2011. The gas and gasohol tax currently produces about two-thirds of the fund's total revenues (see Table 2). The second largest source is the levy of 24.3 cents per gallon on diesel, which accounts for about one-quarter of the revenues. Thus, taxes on motor fuels generate about 90 percent of the trust fund's total revenues. The rest come from a retail sales tax on certain trucks, a tax on the use of certain heavy vehicles, and a tax on truck tires. About 2.8 cents per gallon of all fuel taxes credited to the Highway Trust Fund is dedicated to the mass transit account, or about 13 percent of all trust fund revenues. That account received about $4.9 billion in 2006.

History of the Highway Trust Fund's Revenues and Spending

The Highway Trust Fund was established in 1956. Since then, there have been several notable changes to the program, including the addition of an account dedicated to transit programs in 1983. Since 1983, many further changes have been made to the highway program, to the taxes dedicated to the Highway Trust Fund, and to trust fund operations. One of the most significant changes occurred in the Taxpayer Relief Act of 1997, which increased amounts deposited into the trust fund by 4.3 cents per gallon of gasoline sold, in addition to the 14.0 cents per gallon previously allocated to the fund.[5]

Table 1. Major Components of the Highway Trust Fund, 2007

(Billions of dollars)	Estimated Receipts[a]	Budget Authority and Obligation Limitations[b]	Estimated Outlays
Highway Account			
Federal-Aid Highway program	n.a.	39.8	33.7
Motor carrier safety	n.a.	0.5	0.5
Highway traffic safety	n.a.	0.8	0.6
Other	n.a.	0	0.2
Subtotal	34.1	41.1	35.0
Mass Transit Account			
Discretionary grants	n.a.	0	0.1
Trust fund share of transit programs[c]	n.a.	7.3	3.6
Subtotal	5.0	7.3	3.7
Total, Highway Trust Fund	39.1	48.3	38.6

Source: Congressional Budget Office.

Notes: n.a. = not applicable.

Numbers may not add up to totals because of rounding.

a. Receipts are deposited in the highway and mass transit accounts but are not earmarked for specific components.

b. Obligation limitations enacted in appropriation acts limit the amount of budget authority available to most Highway Trust Fund programs. The amounts in this column are the sum of obligation limitations and budget authority that is not subject to any such limitation.

c. Includes only outlays from 2007 funds. Outlays from previous years' funding were recorded in those years as transfers to other budget accounts.

Over the past 15 years, spending for programs funded through the Highway Trust Fund has increased as a share of nondefense spending. Over the 1992–1996 period, spending from the trust fund was about 1.8 percent of nondefense spending; over the past five years, it has increased to 2.1 percent (see Table 3). When considered as a percentage of GDP, spending from the trust fund has also increased.

Table 2. Estimated Highway Trust Fund Revenues, 2006

(Billions of				
Revenue Source	Tota l	Highway Account	Mass Transit Account	Percentage of Total Trust Fund Revenues
Gasoline Tax	24.9	21.0	3.9	64
Diesel Tax	9.6	8.5	1.1	25
Tax on Trucks and	3.6	3.6	0	9
Use Tax on Certain	1.1	1.1	0	3
Truck Tire Tax	0.5	0.5	0	1
Refunds[a]	-0.9	-0.8	-0.1	-2
Total	**38.8**	**33.9**	**4.9**	**100**

Source: Congressional Budget Office.

a. Section 9503(c) of the Internal Revenue Code provides for refunds from the Highway Trust Fund to be paid out for fuel used for certain nontaxable purposes. Those include, but are not limited to, vehicles operated by state and local governments, certain nonhighway vehicles, local transit systems, and vehicles used on farms.

Table 3. Spending from the Highway Trust Fund over Selected Periods, 1992 to 2006

(Billions of dollars)	1992-1996	1997-2001	2002-2006
Average Spending from the Highway Trust Fund	21.6	28.9	38.9
As a percentage of nondefense spending	1.8	2.0	2.1
As a percentage of gross domestic product	0.31	0.32	0.34
Memorandum:			
Average Nondefense Spending	1,184	1,439	1,873
Average Gross Domestic Product	6,959	9,141	11,606

Source: Congressional Budget Office.

Spending from the trust fund started increasing rapidly in 1999, resulting from changes enacted in the Transportation Equity Act for the 21st Century (TEA-21), which provided budget authority and contract authority of $218 billion over the 1998–2003 period (an average of $36.3 billion per year).

Consequently, annual outlays rose by 40 percent from 1999 to 2003. SAFETEA-LU, which provided contract authority of $286 billion (an average of $57.2 billion per year) over the 2005–2009 period, represented a further significant increase in funding over previous authorizations.

Balances in the highway account were steady during the 1980s and the first half of the 1990s, in the vicinity of $10 billion. Receipts substantially exceeded outlays from 1996 to 2000, and the unexpended balance in the highway account (sometimes called the cash balance) grew from $10 billion in 1995 to a peak of about $23 billion in 2000 (see Figure 3). Revenues fell sharply in 2001, but have increased steadily since then—at an average rate of about 3.4 percent per year through 2007.[6] Nevertheless, spending, boosted by TEA-21, has generally exceeded revenues since 2001. As a result, unspent balances in the highway account declined to about $8.0 billion by the end of 2007. In general, balances in the mass transit account also have been falling since 2000, although at a slower rate than those in the highway account. At the end of 2007, the balance in the mass transit account totaled about $7.9 billion

Appropriations from the General Fund for Transit Programs and Emergency Relief

A portion of transit spending is appropriated from the general fund. From 1998 (and the enactment of TEA-2 1) to 2006, transit programs have received about $18 billion in general fund appropriations, or about $2 billion per year. (Such general fund appropriations totaled about 30 percent of the contract authority for transit programs over the same time period.) By far, the largest component of such appropriations is the Capital Investment Grants (CIG) program, which accounted for about $10 billion of that spending over the 1998–2006 period. The CIG program provides capital assistance for certain programs to create, expand, or modernize certain rail, bus, and ferry facilities. The second largest component of such appropriations—about $7 billion—was a program of formula grants for transit operations that has been funded through the Highway Trust Fund since 2005. Appropriations from the general fund also pay for research programs and administrative expenses of transit programs.

Since 2005, certain appropriations for FHWA's Emergency Relief program have come from the general fund. That program provides for the reconstruction of certain highways and bridges that have suffered serious damage as a result of natural disasters or catastrophic failures from an external cause. Annually, $100 million is set aside in the Highway Trust Fund for such programs. Before 2005, additional budget authority was appropriated from the trust fund as needed. From 1999 to 2004, such appropriations totaled more than $3 billion. However, starting in 2005, the Congress has appropriated additional money for emergency relief from the general fund: about $4.3 billion since that year.

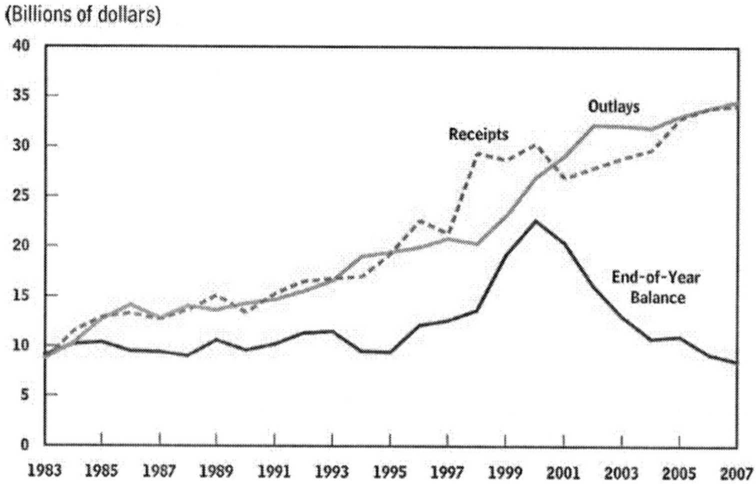

Source: Congressional Budget Office.

Figure 3. Receipts, Outlays, and Balances of the Highway Account, 1983 to 2007.

PROJECTIONS OF THE HIGHWAY TRUST FUND'S REVENUES AND SPENDING

The status of the Highway Trust Fund is generally assessed by projecting the balances in it, which indicate whether the expected revenues will be sufficient to cover the anticipated spending. Those balances represent the cumulative difference between revenues and outlays over the life of the fund and indicate how much the fund has available, at any particular time, to meet its current and future obligations.

The Highway Trust Fund's Balances

CBO has estimated the trust fund's future balances by projecting revenues and outlays independently of each other because they have different bases. Revenues depend on the collection of various taxes, and outlays depend on the obligation limitations set in appropriation acts as well as the timing of spending for obligations that have been made in prior years. For those projections, CBO assumes that policymakers will continue to control spending through such limitations. Further, for the purpose of these estimates, the agency assumes that appropriation acts will set obligation limitations equal to the amounts specified in SAFETEA-LU plus any adjustments for what is termed revenue-aligned budget authority (RABA), a funding mechanism contained in the 2005 law that is designed to strengthen the relationship between the highway account's revenues and spending.[7]

Projections of Highway Trust Fund Revenues

If the current taxes are extended beyond their 2011 expiration date, revenues credited to the Highway Trust Fund will rise at an average annual rate of about 2 percent per year over the coming decade, CBO projects. Total trust fund revenues will grow from about $39 billion in 2006 to about $40 billion in 2009—at a slower rate than nominal GDP, which CBO expects to rise at an average annual rate of 4.6 percent over the next 10 years. (In large part, the difference exists because fuel tax collections depend on the quantity of fuel consumed rather than on the price of gasoline.) As a result, trust fund revenues are projected to decline from 0.25 percent of GDP in 2007 to 0.19 percent of GDP in 2017 if the current taxes are extended.

Projections of Highway Trust Fund Outlays

CBO bases its estimates of trust fund outlays primarily on historical spending patterns, which reflect states' multiyear projects to plan and build roads, bridges, and other transportation infrastructure. In the case of the fund's highway account, most of the obligations involve capital projects on which money is spent over a number of years. For example, the Federal-Aid Highway program typically spends about 27 percent of its budgetary resources in the year they are made available for spending and the rest over the next several years. Most of the highway programs' existing obligations will therefore be met using future tax revenues because those obligations far exceed the amounts now in the account. At the end of fiscal year 2007, the balance of the highway account stood at $8.0 billion, whereas the outstanding obligations of highway programs totaled about $45 billion.

If lawmakers set obligation limitations at the amounts authorized in SAFETEALU and add RABA adjustments (as estimated by CBO), outlays from the trust fund's highway account will gradually increase from about $35.0 billion in 2007 to about $42 billion in 2009, CBO estimates, if amounts in the trust fund are sufficient. Those outlays would exceed revenues by $5 billion in 2008 and more than $6 billion in 2009. In addition, CBO anticipates that about $2 billion from the highway account will be transferred to the mass transit account over that period.[8] By CBO's estimates, balances in the highway account will be exhausted during fiscal year 2009, falling short of amounts needed to meet estimated obligations coming due in that year by $4 billion to $5 billion, or about 10 percent of the projected spending.

For projections of outlays after 2009, CBO assumes that SAFETEA-LU spending levels grow at the rate of inflation, a practice consistent with the agency's usual procedures for baseline projections. Under that assumption, the differential between revenues and projected outlays would be larger in 2010 and beyond (see Figure 4). Under an assumption that revenues remain at projected levels through 2017, outlays from the highway account, if unconstrained, would exceed revenues by a total of about $67 billion (or 17 percent) over the 2009–2017 period.

Under SAFETEA-LU and including transfers from the highway account, the obligation limit for mass transit would grow from $8.3 billion in 2007 to $9.4 billion in 2009. By CBO's estimates, outlays would exceed revenues by about $500 million in 2008 and by almost $2 billion in 2009. With obligation limits adjusted for inflation after 2009, the mass transit account would have sufficient resources to meet estimated spending until 2012, according to CBO's estimates. Subsequently, CBO estimates, projected spending from the transit account would exceed estimated receipts by $3 billion to $4 billion a year.

CBO's projections of the rate of spending from the trust fund are based on historical averages, but those rates might vary from year to year in accordance with factors such as states' construction schedules and plans. Also, changes in oil prices, the economy, and the fuel efficiency of vehicles can all cause future revenues to differ from CBO's projections. Small deviations from those projections would not significantly affect the future status of the Highway Trust Fund and the expected imbalance between obligations and resources.

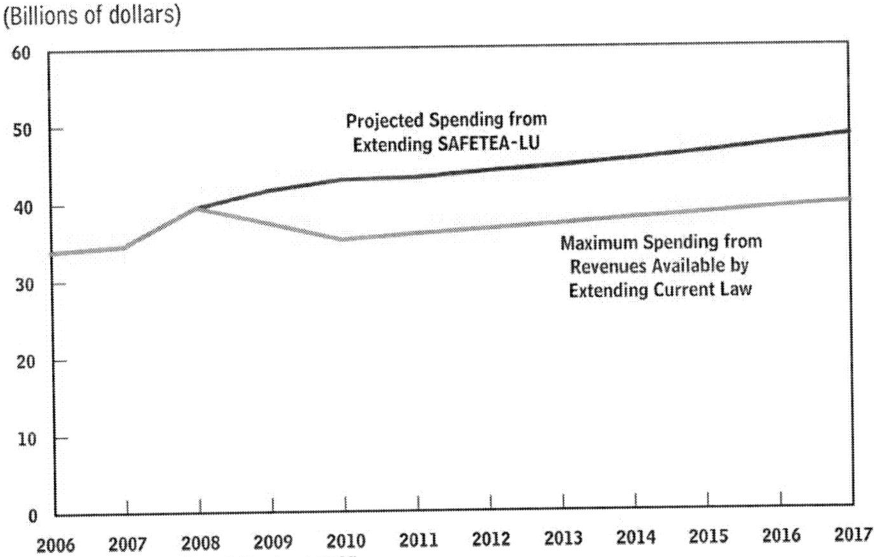

Source: Congressional Budget Office.

Note: Projections in the figure assume that spending authority under the Safe, Accountable, Flexible, Efficient Transportation Equity Act: A Legacy for Users (SAFETEA-LU) grows at the rate of inflation after 2009; the estimated maximum spending from the highway account reflects what could be sustained by projected revenues.

Figure 4. Projected Spending from Extending SAFETEA-LU Compared with the Maximum Spending That Could Be Sustained from Revenues Credited to the Highway Account of the Highway Trust Fund.

Options to Address the Differential in the Highway Account between Expected Revenues and Projected Spending

If the balances in the highway account fell to zero, the Administration would have to take some action to constrain spending because the trust fund is not authorized to borrow money or to incur negative balances.

Possible Actions by the Administration

Without a change to current law, CBO anticipates that by 2009 the Administration will need to act to remedy the imbalance between revenues and outlays in the trust fund—probably by constraining the use of contract authority. Although the Administration has not yet stated how it will address that eventuality, a variety of options exist. The Department of Transportation may have to suspend the current practice of immediately reimbursing states for spending on highway programs and, instead, require states to wait for reimbursement until additional receipts are credited to the trust fund. At that time, the Administration may choose to reimburse states on a "first-in, first-out" basis. The Administration could also use the Emergency Relief program as a model and divide the available funds among all states requesting reimbursement, or it could develop another way to allocate the resources in the trust fund.

Legislative Options to Reduce the Difference between Revenues and Spending

To balance revenues and spending, lawmakers could reduce future obligation limitations and budget authority below the levels assumed in CBO's projections, increase revenues to accommodate future spending levels, or pursue a combination of the two. The examples below provide some of many alternatives available to the Congress.

Reducing Outlays

One option available to lawmakers is to reduce federal spending on highway programs. To do so, the Congress would need to cut the obligation limitations that control spending on those programs. For example, to constrain outlays to the revenues available in 2009, lawmakers would need to reduce the obligation limitation for that year in SAFETEA-LU by about $16 billion—roughly a 40 percent decrease. Subsequently, relative to obligation limitations growing at the rate of inflation, cuts in those limitations would need to average about $9 billion annually from 2010 through 2017, for a total of $79 billion over the 2009– 2017 period—a reduction of about 20 percent.[9]

Increasing Revenues

To maintain spending on highway programs at SAFETEALU levels, the Congress could choose to raise additional revenues through an increase in the gas tax or through other mechanisms. According to estimates from the Joint Committee on Taxation, a one-cent increase in the gas tax, effective October 1, 2008, would raise slightly less than $2 billion for the trust fund annually over the next 10 years.[10] About 87 percent of those funds accrue to the highway account.

CBO estimates that receipts to the highway account in 2009 will total $35.3 billion. To cover all obligations that will probably come due that year if they continue at SAFETEA-LU levels, revenues credited to that account would have to increase by between $4 billion and $5 billion. A gas tax increase of about 3 cents per gallon of fuel sold would raise that amount for the highway account and about $600 million for the transit account.

Over the 2010–2017 period, with increases in obligation rates assumed to reflect inflation, revenues credited to the highway account would have to be about 20 percent, or $8 billion, above current projections for each year, to meet obligations that would become due in each year. To generate such a sum for the highway account, revenues would need to increase by about $9 billion per year, requiring an increase in the gas tax of about 5 cents per gallon, effective October 1, 2010.[11] Resulting increases in revenues to the mass transit account, about $1 billion per year, would maintain positive balances in that fund until 2014.

A Combination of Reducing Outlays and Increasing Revenues

Lawmakers could also choose to both reduce spending and increase revenues. For example, if the Congress chose to decrease spending from the highway account by 10 percent (relative to SAFETEA-LU levels inflated)—about $40 billion—over the 2009–2017 period, revenues would also have to increase by about 10 percent compared with the level in CBO's projections. Of that increase, under current law about $34 billion would be credited to the highway account and $5 billion to the mass transit account. A gas tax increase of about 2.5 cents per gallon of fuel sold, beginning in 2009, would generate such a revenue stream.

FUTURE FUNDING OF TRANSPORTATION INFRASTRUCTURE

By many indications, the nation's surface transportation system will require substantial investments in coming decades. The number of vehicle-miles traveled has been growing by about 2 percent a year, and trucks are carrying increasing amounts of freight. As a result, congestion is growing; the Department of Transportation projects that traffic on a substantial percentage of the Interstate Highway System will exceed its capacity by 2020. The department recently estimated that $78.8 billion per year (in 2004 dollars) will be needed over the next 20 years to maintain the nation's highway system in its current condition, and another $15.8 billion will be needed to maintain transit systems in their current condition.

Empirical research indicates that, as a whole, public investment in transportation infrastructure makes a positive contribution to the economy, but determining the appropriate level of government spending on that infrastructure is difficult. For example, identifying the amount of spending necessary is difficult at the aggregate level because individual infrastructure projects have varying costs and benefits depending upon their age, type of construction, intensity of use, and other factors. Economic returns from infrastructure will also vary significantly among projects because those returns depend upon a number of factors, including the amount of infrastructure already in place. For example, analysts have found that the initial construction of the Interstate Highway System from the late-1950s through early-1970s increased the productivity of those industries relying on the nation's roadways to acquire materials and distribute their products. Subsequent investments to expand or rehabilitate the nation's roads have apparently had a much smaller economic impact, although they provide other important benefits—such as ensuring the safety and reliability of existing infrastructure—that are probably not fully captured by estimates of purely economic returns.

In assessing the future status of the Highway Trust Fund and what actions might be necessary to ensure a balance between its income and spending, it is useful to address the broader questions of what total spending ought to be and what role the federal government ought to play in financing that spending. Some of the relevant questions include:

- Are the funds that the federal government is currently collecting and spending for surface transportation programs going to their best uses?

Could the potential imbalance between the trust fund's revenues and spending be remedied, at least in part, by better targeting spending to its most productive uses? If so, what rules or procedures would be most effective in that regard?

- If more money is raised from transportation-related taxes, what steps ought to be taken to ensure that those funds are used to meet the highest-priority needs?
- What is the appropriate role for the federal government in the financing of transportation infrastructure? If more money is needed, should the federal government raise taxes to collect it, or should states, which ultimately determine how most of the funds are spent, bear the responsibility for imposing and collecting the necessary taxes or fees? If the federal government collects the money, how much flexibility should states have in determining how to spend the federal dollars?
- To what extent does federal funding substitute for spending that would otherwise be undertaken by other levels of government?
- What is the appropriate role for the private sector in the financing of transportation infrastructure? Should the federal government facilitate a greater private- sector role, and if so, how?

The answers to those questions are not necessarily clear or straightforward, but they are relevant in determining funding and financing strategies for the surface transportation system.

FINANCING TRANSPORTATION INFRASTRUCTURE

In assessing ways to finance transportation spending—whether at the federal level or at the state and local levels—it is useful to consider not only how much various financing approaches might raise but also what kinds of incentives they provide to users of the transportation system. There is a strong rationale for charging users for the costs of transportation infrastructure because they reap substantial benefits that the system provides. Designing and implementing a financing system that charges users of transportation infrastructure for the costs that they impose on the system can encourage efficient use of existing roads, rails, and other transportation infrastructure. It can also help in identifying needs and paying for the construction of new infrastructure in the right places at the right time. The charges users pay for the costs that they impose on the system provide a measure of the value of investment in increased capacity.

The Current System

Under the current system, receipts from various excise taxes, most notably those on the sale of gasoline, diesel, and other motor fuels, are collected and credited to the Highway Trust Fund. The Congress determines how much money each state receives from the fund. Most of that determination reflects existing apportionment formulas provided in law, but some spending is based on specific allocations to states in legislation. The formulas determine which types of projects are undertaken, but each state determines which specific projects to undertake. The federal government then reimburses states from the Highway Trust Fund for the federal share of those projects.

The current system for funding bridges and roads collects the funds used for that infrastructure from users of the system, though not always in proportion to the costs they impose on the system. The fuel taxes, which CBO estimates funded about 90 percent of federal highway spending in 2006, are partially related to the wear and tear that driving inflicts on roads, bridges, and other transportation infrastructure. For example, vehicles that travel farther burn more fuel and pay more in taxes. Heavier vehicles that do more damage to pavement and bridges also burn more fuel and pay more in taxes, but probably not in proportion to the damage they cause. For example, a heavily loaded truck uses somewhat more fuel and pays somewhat more in taxes than a comparatively light automobile but does much greater damage to pavement and bridges. However, the current system is also demonstrably workable. Collection costs are low, and evading the taxes is difficult.

The long-run economic viability of the existing financing system is in question, however. Existing taxes on gasoline, diesel fuel, and ethanol are a fixed number of cents per gallon and thus do not increase with inflation. However, construction costs continue to rise. The Federal Highway Administration's Composite Bid Price Index, which measures contract prices for goods and services commonly used in highway construction, increased by 74 percent since the enactment of TEA-21 in 1998.[12] That average annual increase is over 7 percent, which is well above other broader measures of inflation, such as the change in the Consumer Price Index. The increase in construction prices contributes to the long-term decline in the purchasing power of revenues accruing to the Highway Trust Fund. For example, the 2006 revenues credited to the highway account are 47 percent more than the 1998 revenues in dollar terms, but those revenues provide about 15 percent less in purchasing power for highway construction. Policymakers could choose to restore the Highway Trust Fund's purchasing power by indexing fuel taxes to account for inflation. But even so, increased fuel efficiency, hybrid vehicles, or alternative fuels could serve to limit the trust fund's receipts in the future.

In addition, current taxes do not account for the costs of pollution and congestion caused by driving. For example, a driver on a congested road uses a little more fuel and pays a little more in taxes than he or she would driving on an uncongested road but imposes much greater costs on other drivers in terms of delay.

Alternatives Based on Charges to Users of Transportation Infrastructure

The federal government, as well as states and localities, could choose to replace or supplement existing fuel taxes with taxes or user fees intended to both recover more of the costs imposed by users of transportation infrastructure and to charge specific users fees that are more directly in line with the costs of their use. A number of such fees already exist in the current financing system at the state and local levels. Widespread use of some such systems may not be practical in the short term, but they might be worth considering over the longer term, particularly if technological developments continue to make them more feasible.

Mileage-based road use fees charge users specifically for road use. Because such fees can vary by location, vehicle type, and time of day, they have the capability to closely match the actual costs imposed by specific users. One form of such fees that are already commonly used on major highway facilities, tolls can be economically efficient because they can vary by vehicle type and therefore can reflect the costs imposed by various classes of vehicles. Many tolls vary by time of day and therefore can reflect the congestion costs imposed on other users. It has long been recognized that tolls that reflect the costs users impose on the system provide a measure of the value of investment in increased capacity.[13] However, the administrative costs of collecting some tolls could be higher than the administrative costs of collecting current motor fuel taxes. Moreover, because tolls currently apply only to some major roads, relying solely on tolls from those roads would not be efficient, equitable, or adequate to pay for the entire highway system.

In response to concerns about the long-term viability of fuel taxes, some states are currently studying the feasibility of mileage-based user fees that apply to all roads, not just major highways. For example, Oregon recently conducted a one-year experiment in which drivers paid a mileage-based fee instead of fuel taxes when they filled up at the gas station. The fee was intended to replace the fuel tax as the primary source of revenues for the state's roads, as well as incorporating congestion pricing based on both location and time of travel. In addition, the state of Washington recently evaluated a system using global positioning system (GPS) technology in vehicles. Drivers were charged different prices per mile depending on both the location and time of travel, thereby incorporating congestion pricing. Expanded use of such systems would overcome some of the practical difficulties of collecting tolls over a broad system of roads but would require addressing other considerations—for example, many cars do not yet have GPS systems—and resolving varied privacy concerns about the government having access to data about who was driving when and where.

Generalized mileage-based fees for the use of roads have several attractive characteristics. Because the fees can vary by vehicle type, time of day, and location, they have the capability to closely match the actual costs that users impose on the system. The fees are equitable for the various classes of users because revenues are raised in proportion to the costs imposed. They send price signals to drivers about the costs that they impose on the system, thus helping to reduce demand, and to transportation planners about the value of adding capacity, thus promoting long- run efficiency. However, while increasing use of electronic monitoring and payment systems has reduced transactions costs, there are still unresolved questions about the degree to which generalized mileage-based road-use charges are technically and administratively feasible when applied to large, complex road systems.

Weight-distance fees charge vehicles based on their weight and configuration of axles and annual miles traveled. Those user fees can be economically efficient at recovering infrastructure costs because vehicles pay in direct proportion to the estimated wear and tear they cause on infrastructure. Consequently, different classes of vehicles are treated equitably. However, weight-distance fees do not reflect congestion costs. A heavy vehicle currently pays the same weight-distance fee whether it travels on a congested road or an uncongested road. Furthermore, weight-distance fees may be more difficult to administer and easier to evade than charges under the current system. While 11 states had weight-distance fees in 1989, today only four states (Kentucky, New Mexico, New York, and Oregon) have them.

Congestion fees charge drivers for the delay that their choice to drive imposes on other drivers. Such fees are higher in times or places with heavy traffic, lower in times or places with light traffic. They are already used at a variety of highways, bridges, and tunnels throughout the United States.[14] For example, on State Route 91 in Orange County, California, congestion fees vary hour to hour in order to maintain a free flow of traffic in the priced lanes. The fees promote efficient use of existing infrastructure by allocating it those who value it most (namely, those most willing to pay the charge). They are also efficient at reducing congestion costs because each vehicle pays for the delay caused to other users. To the extent that some drivers choose to use other modes or routes or to travel at less congested times of the day rather than pay the fee, congestion is reduced. Congestion fees also send price signals about the need to add capacity, thus promoting long-run efficiency. Electronic technology makes the fees inexpensive to administer on the largest, most congested roads. In many recent applications of congestion pricing, such as I-3 94 outside Minneapolis, Minnesota, overhead sensors read electronic transponders in vehicles, eliminating the need for drivers to stop or even slow down. Moreover, London and Stockholm have successfully imposed charges on driving in the center of those cities to reduce congestion.

Congestion fees have some drawbacks. It may not be equitable to have users of congested roads pay some or all of the cost of the road system while users of uncongested roads pay little or none. In addition, charging high tolls could raise concerns about the impact on low-income users. Last, the administrative feasibility of congestion fees in a broad variety of applications found throughout the highway system is not yet clear.

End Notes

[1] Additional detail on infrastructure spending is available in Congressional Budget Office, *Trends in Public Spending on Transportation and Water Infrastructure,* 1956 to 2004 (August 2007). Supplemental data tables and a methodological appendix include data sources and definitions. The paper addresses public spending on surface transportation and other types of infrastructure: aviation, water resources (such as dams and levees), and water supply and wastewater treatment. Public spending on all transportation and water infrastructure in 2004 was $312 billion, in 2006 dollars.

[2] State and local spending on operation and maintenance reflects in part conditions that the federal government places on grants and loan subsidies that it provides. Those funds often may not be used for those purposes.

[3] Those federal outlays for infrastructure do not include several types of financial support for infrastructure: first, the revenues forgone by the federal government through the tax exemptions on income from bonds issued by state and local governments to finance infrastructure and, second, sizable outlays by the Department of Homeland Security to protect infrastructure. See Congressional Budget Office, *Trends in Public Spending on Transportation and Water Infrastructure*.

[4] Other agencies within the Department of Transportation also receive funding from the Highway Trust Fund, including the Federal Motor Carriers Administration and the National Highway Transportation Safety Administration. In 2007, the Federal Motor Carriers Administration and the National Highway Transportation Safety Administration received a total of about 3 percent of the budgetary resources from the Highway Trust Fund.

[5] The total gas tax is 18.4 cents per gallon. Of that, 18.3 cents is deposited in the Highway Trust Fund, and 0.1 cents goes to the Leaking Underground Storage Trust Fund. (The 1993 Omnibus Budget and Reconciliation Act increased the gas tax by 4.3 cents; the added receipts were not initially deposited into the trust fund, but into the general fund of the Treasury.)

[6] Revenues recorded to the Highway Trust Fund were especially strong in 2005, following changes in the tax treatment of certain fuels. The American Jobs Creation Act of 2004 modified the subsidy for ethanol production by establishing a tax credit paid from the Treasury's general fund. That credit replaced a lower tax rate for gasoline containing ethanol. The law also included other provisions to increase revenues to the Highway Trust Fund.

[7] That assumption differs from the one underlying CBO's baseline budget projections, which are governed by the rules set forth in the Balanced Budget and Emergency Deficit Control Act. In its most recent baseline, CBO projected highway spending over the next decade by assuming that the budget authority and obligation limitations in future years would equal those enacted in the 2007 appropriation act for the Department of Transportation, adjusted for inflation. With that projection method, baseline funding levels for highways are lower than the levels specified in SAFETEA-LU.

[8] Under SAFETEA-LU, states are allowed to use some of their highway funds for transit projects; funds are transferred from the highway account to the transit account when states choose to use such flexibility.

[9] Because the spending that is estimated to occur each year is only partly from new spending authority, that authority would need to be reduced substantially in 2009 to ensure a sufficient reduction in spending in that year.

[10] Because excise taxes reduce the tax base of income and payroll taxes, higher excise taxes would lead to reductions in income and payroll tax revenues. The estimates shown here do not reflect those reductions. Those reductions would amount to an estimated 25 percent of the estimated increase in excise tax receipts.

[11] All revenue estimates are provided by the Joint Committee on Taxation.

[12] Federal Highway Administration, *Price Trends for Highway Construction*, Fourth Quarter, 2006.

[13] See William S. Vickery, "Congestion Theory and Transport Investment," *American Economic Review*, vol. 59, no. 2, (May 1969), pp. 259–260.

[14] For a list of current and planned congestion-pricing projects, see Federal Highway Administration, Office of Transportation Management, *Value Pricing Project Quarterly Reports,* available at http://ops.fhwa.dot.gov/tolling_pricing/value_pricing/quarterlyreport/index.htm.

Chapter Sources

The following chapters have been previously published:

Chapter 1 – This is an edited, reformatted and augmented version of a United States Government Accountability Office, Report to Congressional Requesters, GAO-08-400 dated March 2008.

Chapter 2 – These remarks were delivered as testimony given on July, 10, 2008. Jayetta Z. Hecker, Director, Physical Infrastructure Issues, before the Committee on Finance, United States Senate.

Chapter 3 – These remarks were delivered as testimony given on October 25, 2007. Robert A Sunshine, Deputy Director, Public Spending on Surface Transportation Infrastructure, before the Committee on the Budget, United States House of Representatives.

INDEX

A

B

C

D

E

F

G

H

I

N

O

P

T

U

V

W

Y